Open-Eyed Sneeze

Open-Eyed Sneeze

A Ridiculous Memoir

Jess Martin

ACKNOWLEDGEMENTS:

Cover design by Geoffrey Gavett
Geoffreygavett.com

Thank you to the following people for their support, enthusiasm, talents, feedback, kindness, and friendship:
Meredith Kendra
Sabrina Martin
Vanessa Martin
Katie Kurcz
Janna Whitney Moss
Kathryn Kaiser
Molly Galler
My Grandma
Every person who ever read my blog.

For my family.
There when I laugh, there when I cry. Usually responsible for both.

A PIT OF BALLS IN RENTED CAP AND GOWN

My worldview was shaped by "The Balls" at Chuck E. Cheese. How I perceive my place in the world in relation to others and the ways in which I attempt to find meaning can be traced back to a pit of primary-colored plastic balls. I would have hoped for something more poetic, but what can you do?

Surrounded by rubber padding and mesh netting so that participants could neither injure themselves nor escape, The Balls (as far as I know they didn't have another name) served as my earliest source of true confusion, and thus, my first attempt to make sense of something. In or out of a pit of balls, looking for significance in what surrounds us is what we're all doing all the time. It's just nice that as children we had the option of throwing stuff at each other while trying to figure it out. Since those days of sensory overload, synthetic material, and uncertainty, the events of my life have essentially been variations on a ball pit theme. Namely, finding myself in absurd situations and hoping to discover value therein.

When I was young, every time we went to Chuck E. Cheese I waited with all the other greasy pizza-hand kids for my turn inside the pit. The only rule was that shoes were not allowed, but once inside there was a no holds barred atmosphere. I spent the time standing in line observing my peers, trying to figure out what exactly I was supposed to do. Obviously, throwing balls at each other was quite popular. Climbing the mesh netting and jumping into the balls was also a big hit. But there were always a few kids whose chosen activities in the balls made me, a six-year-old, furrow my brow in confusion. Most six-year-olds have a "Why can't I wear a cape to church?" furrow. I had more of a, "What the hell are you doing?" furrow. I was mystified by the kids who jumped in and started flailing about like it was their first time in the deep end, kicking furiously, moving their heads quickly side to side, cupping their hands under and digging through the balls. And then, some other kid in the corner, probably the sibling of the nervous freak trying to stay afloat, would hold his nose and dive under. By the time my turn came I hadn't a single clue what to do. I simply took off my shoes, hopped in, got pegged in the face a few times, and came out missing a sock.

Fifteen years later, here I am, still unsure about what's going on and looking to the people in front of me for guidance. I'm hot and itchy and these $19.99 sandals have already caused blisters. All cheap sandals should come with a label on the sole that reads, "You Have No One To Blame But Yourself." When all this is over my first move as an adult will be to swear off inexpensive footwear. And maybe do something about this persistent sweating problem. Damn it. I cannot stop sweating.

I think I have a rare pituitary disorder that causes me to sweat in social situations, or celebrations, or venues where cake is served or cards are exchanged. Basically any event with an expectation of memory formation causes me to perspire. My sweat glands are probably just trying to make up for the rest of my body's disinterest. I appreciate what certain events stand for, but I just get so overwhelmed by the proceedings leading up to the event that I can't remember feeling a single emotion. I can remember sweating profusely, but they don't make greeting cards about sweat.

I've learned that if a greeting card can be bought for it, the moment will probably be lost on me. I don't like to think that times can be defined by rhyming stanzas or that clever cartoons could somehow enhance the memory. And that most people use them in lieu of actually saying anything, almost completely negates all meaning. "You've had a child. This bird wearing pants has something to say about that. I hope this displays how important you are to me and how happy I am for you."

My mother loves cards. My older sister Sabrina loves cards. Every year since I can remember Sabrina has given my mother a card that has made her cry. Birthdays, holidays, and anniversaries are all occasions to seal tears in a colored envelope. When my mother reads a card and inevitably cries, Sabrina inhales deeply and sort of puffs up with pride looking to me and my younger sister Vanessa with a gentle smile, as if to say, "Beat that." I always look at her flatly with absolutely no pride, inhaled or otherwise, as if to say, "I can't. I didn't even buy a card. My birthday present to mom is to not make her cry. But nice job with yours."

Today is my college graduation. The card aisle of the grocery store tells me this is an event. That in itself is enough to turn me off to the whole thing.

Perhaps this void of emotion on days of importance stems from my early experiences surrounding 'occasions.' When we were kids and my parents went out on a date together, it was always a big deal. My father's job on his farm rarely allowed for such a treat and as a result our house was turned into backstage at Radio City in the hours leading up to their dinner and a movie. Buying new outfits and cutting off the tags, the roar of blow dryers, and the steam from the bathroom; if you listened carefully during these times, you'd hear my mother's battle cry. She lives for this shit. I—in a word—don't.

3

Sabrina used to help my mom accessorize and line up her makeup while Vanessa would put one of my mother's bras on over her pajamas and walk around yelling, "Fashion show!" I would always be in the living room watching TV waiting to be "Breath Tester." Once they were both ready to leave, my mother would bend down and say, "Smell my breath. Hah, hah," breathing twice on my face. Middle children have forever been breath testers. But that combined smell of Scope and lipstick told me we would soon be eating babysitter food of chicken nuggets and crinkle cut fries. As a result, all this preparation for special occasions ever created in me was a craving for frozen foods and an aversion to being breathed on.

Bill Clinton is delivering the commencement speech about 100 yards away from where I'm sitting and I can't hear a single word he says. The acoustics in the Dome, Syracuse's enclosed stadium, are horrible so I'm passing the time playing Snake on my cell phone. I wonder what he's talking about. He's probably just saying the same things people said at the School of Communications ceremony yesterday. But come to think of it, I wasn't paying attention to those speeches either. That was such a weird spectacle yesterday, watching my fellow classmates walk one by one to receive an empty diploma holder. The ceremony just served as a reminder of my apprehension toward waiting in line for established activities. If you were going to do something, fine. But standing there, waiting for everyone else to do it, gave you too much time to see the ridiculousness of the whole thing. Think pit of balls, in rented cap and gown. Damn, it's really hot in here. I hand my phone to a friend so he can try to beat my high score and I pull at my robe while slowly scanning the stage. The faculty members, dressed like they're attending a Harry Potter convention, look just as uncomfortable as I feel. This is a benchmark moment in my life and three things are standing out in my mind: Cheap sandal blister pain, the swamp-like atmosphere I've created under this robe, and the giant mess my family made in my apartment this morning that I'll need to clean up after packing my things.

Any time there is an event in my family—and an event is defined by whether or not my mother has mints in her purse—there are added and always unnecessary dramatics. It begins with lists and scheduling and multiple phone calls to insure that these things are as confusing as possible. For example, a message leading up to today could be very similar to this:

"Hi Jess, it's Mom. Listen, call me back with the name of the restaurant you'd like to go to after and I'll make reservations. Also, I've made a list of things I'll bring when we come so don't worry about buying them. So far I have bobby pins, extra panty hose, cameras, nail polish, and we'll bring breakfast beforehand so don't worry about that. Did I say bobby pins? Ok, call me back if I'm forgetting anything."

Bobby pins are another huge event definer. I never took dance lessons but my mom has responded to anything I've ever done in my life as if attending a recital.

The family arrived at 5:30 this morning with all of their clothes for the graduation and bags of bagels and coffee, spilling creamers and sesame seeds everywhere and using the bathroom multiple times, I think just to upset me. My mom brought fans from home because my place doesn't have AC and with everyone getting ready at the same time the power kept going out. I had to reset the fuse and restart my computer four different times to ensure my "graduating from college. brb" away message stayed posted online. I opened gifts, which included a giant stuffed mascot that screamed "Let's Go Orange" when you pushed its hand, but that broke after one use and continued to play for the five hours we spent around my place. It's awkward when you have to bury a gift under a pile of blankets. "No, I love it! Thank You!" And then fight the eye roll as you hear the chant from beneath the velux. Is it me, or don't people usually get cars or trips to Europe after these things? But that's the practical gift-giving of my parents. Nothing says *welcome to the real world* quite like a giant plush toy.

The cheering of the crowd inside the Dome snaps my mind out of its wandering.

I think the ceremony is over. I didn't hear the closing words but people seem excited so I'll take my cues from them. Trying to find my family in the stands for the obligatory photo ops, I run into one of my favorite professors.

Squinting at me like she can barely recognize me she asks, "Jessica, what are you doing here?"

Pulling on my robe I say, "Well you know. I like to get some use out of this thing. Talk about impractical purchases."

"I thought you were a junior?"
"Oh, yeah. Well, I had a lot of credits coming in my freshman year so I was able to finish early."

Shaking her head with concern, she asks with a genuine curiosity, "Why would you do that?"

Standing with widened eyes I think of all the times I've heard that question: Once after sticking my arm through the horn part of my saxophone with predictable results, once after biting down as hard as I could on a Jolly-Rancher so that my teeth stuck together and I couldn't open my mouth, and once after going out of my way to walk atop a five foot snow drift and falling in. Graduating from college doesn't seem to belong on this list of moronic moves. But as soon as she asks, I experience the same feeling as I had all those other times. That sudden flash of heat, a nervous turn of the stomach, a spontaneous combustion of shivers and sweat that cues my brain to ask, "No, seriously?"

Searching for an answer and realizing I didn't have one, I simply ignore the question. An awkward silence ensues, she wishes me well, and I meet my family. My mother is passing out mints to everyone to hold them over until we get to the restaurant and she seems quite pleased with herself. There are easily six tins of Altoids in her purse and I want to comment on the excess, but refrain. I simply watch as she hands my father tin after tin to hold as she searches her bag for the car keys.

Given my position on events it should be no surprise that I'm also not a huge fan of the celebratory meal. There's just something completely anti-climactic about eating out as a means of merriment. Something about waiting 45-minutes for a buzzer to light up, signaling your table is ready, chips away at the festivities. By the time you order and get your food it's basically just another meal out, asking everyone at the table if they'd like to try a bite of your entrée. But restaurant celebratory meals do distinguish themselves in some respects. In my family, all of the following are guaranteed to occur: Pictures, force-feeding, and check placement anticipation anxiety.

Multiple pictures are always taken at the table while everyone is eating, ensuring that none of said photos will ever be framed because, "Oh, you had your fork so close to your face in that one." And any opportunity to enjoy each other's company is interrupted by instructions to smile like you mean it.

My dad will order soup and insist on passing it around despite requests for him not to do so. Before our entrées arrive it's a round of pass the soup until it eventually ends up back with him; he'll taste it, frown slightly and say under his breath, "It's a little cold." That he's genuinely curious as to why this is is the upsetting part.

If my grandma is with us—and for celebrations she usually is—the last twenty minutes of the meal become increasingly distressing. For all the years of my existence my grandma has never allowed anyone but herself to pay for a meal. I've seen her nearly rip limbs off wait staff to take the check. And one time, though I can't be entirely sure, I think she burnt a hole through a chair with the glare from her eyes after my mother offered to pay. So any joy in the post-event celebration meal is trumped by the fear that a waiter might hand the check to my dad.

After pictures and lunch, I return to my apartment for the final pack and clean. I find most of my endings and most of my beginnings share one thing in common—large bags. This occurs to me as I struggle to lift my things in a way that seems vaguely familiar to the first day I came here. Pushing the last of my bags down as far as possible in the back of my father's pickup I ask, "Dad, think maybe we should tie this stuff down?"

Conducting the highly effective test of wiggling the bags he replies, "No, should be okay."

It's hard to put 100% faith in the man's words. My dad seems to think that a powerful magnetic force exists between moving vehicles and the objects they're carrying that defies all laws of physics. Once, an old neighbor asked my dad if we'd like their piano and he seriously debated using a forklift to pick it up and drive it home. "It's only a mile," he reasoned. I imagined him moving down the road at three mph, piano on lift, as a siren and flashing lights came on behind him. "Is there a problem, Officer? Oh, no. I didn't realize this wasn't allowed. Do you play?"

I keep forgetting to ask, but somehow he did get that piano. And now almost everything I owned was driving off with him.

Waving goodbye, I head inside my apartment to pack my remaining things and clean well enough to get my security deposit back. The final cleaning of an apartment is so cold; empty spaces, the strong smell of cleaning product, bare walls, it's all so antiseptic. The naked rooms almost scream at you to leave, saying something about how you don't live there anymore. When your things are cleared out, you can feel the resentment of the rental unit who has seen it all a thousand times before. Without your belongings to build it up, it's reduced to a skeleton of a home and its only defense is to make you feel unwelcome so you'll hurry up and leave. This is the last memory of the place I lived. This bitter space, this Clorox-smelling box, was home.

Running the Swiffer over the floors for the last time, I think, endings are always hardest. Or is it the start? I'm always hearing one of the two but can't seem to remember which one it is. I find myself in the fuzzy area in between, as I lock the door and leave.

A HOMECOMING

I stop counting the cars racing by me after about
fifteen minutes on the New York State Thruway. Moving at
45 mph surely deserves the road rage exhibited by every person who passes, and making eye contact with them as they
verbally abuse me makes my ride all the more uncomfortable. Although, once you've seen thirty consecutive faces of
rage it's hard not to find them humorous. I can clearly make
out the expletives the passing drivers are shouting at me, but
I simply pretend they're eager to know the whereabouts of
the next IHOP exit.

A man lays on his horn and moves his mouth slowly
and with exaggeration, the way that singers and actors warm
up for rehearsal. He looks like a very upset fish the way his
mouth is moving. He's telling me where to go, and where I
can put certain things, and now his finger is involved.

"What's that, partner? Want some pancakes? Oh,
you just want one pancake? Okay, we'll get you a pancake.
Ease up fella, just a few more exits and you're there. Gosh,
by the puss on that face looks like you could use a tall stack.
Maybe get some berries."

Then I realize he's long gone, I'm still moving well
below the speed limit, and now talking to myself, which

is only fodder for the next car telling me off. I believe this series of events may explain the everyday driving experience of the elderly.

Nevertheless, using this technique of oblivion I decide to stop looking at the speedometer and let my fellow drivers scream all they want about pancakes. Normally the trip home would take less than two hours, but something is telling me to take my time with this one.

Drives home never have that movie montage quality for which you'd hope. They're usually full of asshole drivers—like me at the moment—and intense leg cramps that force you to pull over and stretch out at rest stops where you'll inevitably break down and buy a six-dollar cone at TCBY. But you can't stay mad at the price because never once in the history of the world has an angry person eaten an ice cream cone and remained angry. Picture an aggravated face. Now picture that same face trying to lick a twist with rainbow sprinkles. Can't do it. I think instead of sending troops into war zones we should install soft-serve machines. Either that, or trampolines, because it's hard for people to maintain a 'mad at the world' visage when they're trying to scissor kick six feet in the air. These are the great open road ideas I have when driving home, partly to pass the time and partly to keep my mind off the final destination.

It's not that I have anything against my town. It was a great place to grow up and the people are wonderful. But I've always had this visual of God examining His creations from above and coming across Brockport only to tilt His head slightly and shrug His Almighty shoulders. Driving through the main drag, one is reminded how many venues there are to buy a meal for under five dollars. There's something to be said for this, I'm just not sure what it is. I understand the idea behind fast food but am somewhat confused about the aesthetic quality it lends to a community. Neon lights and deep fryers are not words I want to use to describe my hometown.

The fact that the con list for the decision to drive back to my parents' house clearly outweighs the pro isn't lost on me. But when you're 21-years-old and have a lot of packed bags and nowhere to put them, you go home.

Movies never touch on all the unenthusiastic thoughts of the destination that run through your mind on a car ride home. It's usually just a flashy scene with a killer soundtrack. Just some carefree character with her belongings in the backseat singing off key, holding her arm out the window to catch a wave of wind. If I could, I'd let that ride last forever. It used to be that any time a good song came on as I was nearing home, I'd drive down the road for a little while longer to keep listening to it. I'd often pass right by the house. If a series of good songs came on, I wonder if I would have never turned back. With each good song my foot might have grown heavier on the pedal until eventually I was miles from anything I knew. I suppose that's the reason for commercials on the radio, to keep people from driving away.

Time and distance on the highway move in that bizarre REM-like long distance drive kind of way, until I'm slowing to turn onto my road, passing the barns and fields of my family's farm. I don't know how I got here so quickly and I try to remember passing certain landmarks, but can't. I roll up the driveway and shut off the engine right outside the garage in no great rush to leave the car. Putting both my hands back on the steering wheel at the ten and two position, I stare at my knuckles for a minute. Taking one deep breath and releasing it with patience, I grab two big bags and enter through the side door.

I walk in the house to find my grandma cooking in the kitchen. Whenever my Grandma Lorraine visits, she never leaves the kitchen. Picking up restaurant bills and preparing food at all hours are the two big ways she says I love you. In her ideal world we would always be laying around and require constant feeding. I don't think she ever wanted grandchildren. She wanted lions. It used to be that when she flew in from Long Island to see us she would pack frozen meats as her carry-ons. Seriously. It was not uncommon for her to deplane with large frozen turkeys or honey hams. And when we asked her to stop she simply switched to something easier to pack, like deli meat. "What? Cold cuts fit right in the overhead."

Hearing me enter the house, my parents come out to the kitchen clapping. I'd seen them hours ago but they love to clap so they take advantage of opportunities to do so. Apparently, walking and showing you know how to pack are both reasons to put your hands together. He didn't have to say anything but I could sense silent pride in my father as he watched me drag my last two bags through our ranch-style home. Having taken the majority of my belongings that afternoon, he was extremely pleased with himself for avoiding a moving service charge. Growing up surrounded by trucks, he took it as a personal affront if someone suggested calling a moving company.

My old bedroom offers no sign that I had ever been there thanks to my younger sister. Sabrina's old bedroom is now home to three beds, old computers, Rubbermaid boxes full of books and various exercise equipment that had failed to keep our interest. The walls are covered in old posters of early 90's pop groups, movie advertisements, and posters bought at book fairs when we were in first grade. Giraffes and kittens together, gorillas holding kittens, kittens sitting on a rhino — all obviously taken on location in the Serengeti. If there was a poster with a kitten on it, and let's be honest, there always was, we bought it. And for some reason my mother has decided to decorate with them.

Leaving my bags at the door of my old room I move to Vanessa's queen size bed; a sound purchase made with the money my parents gave her to visit me when I studied in London. I believe that conversation went something like:

Mom: You bought a bed?!

Vanessa: Yeah, I'm too old to sleep in bunk beds.

Mom: So the money we gave you to visit your sister?

Vanessa: That's gone.

Dad: You didn't pay for delivery did you?

Crawling onto the bed and crashing with slow motion dramatics onto my stomach, face down between the ends of two pillows to create a little air pocket, arms and legs spread like the Vitruvian Man, the fabric softener smell of the sheets has an immediate calming effect. I have to hand it to my mother. The woman knows the intricacies of an appropriate homecoming. I remember when we were small she would take out towels fresh from the dryer and wrap them around our necks and feet, making us into burritos of freshness. In our harsh upstate New York winters, a load of colors was our eternal spring.

I hear Vanessa coming down the hall and shut my eyes. She wouldn't kick a sleeping person out of her bed. Standing in the doorway having obviously seen my fast attempt to fake-sleep she says, "I know you're not asleep."

"Yes I am." I reply.

"There's a bed in the other room, you know?"

"Yes. There are three actually. Listen, I'm exhausted, this used to be my room, and I'm not sleeping in mini-storage across the hall so I don't know what you want me to do."

"It's fine. I just came to get you for dinner."

If I don't jump out of bed the second Vanessa says dinner it's only because I know I'm too tired to get through another family meal right now. Our dinners together almost always require that I retreat into my mind and allow hallucinations to reign over actual conversation. That way I can pretend that something I hear might have been imagined. I discovered this technique years ago at a Sunday dinner at my great-grandmother's house. My family's signature conversational style was perfected around my great-grandmother's dinner table; a flawless blend of volume, food commentary, and schizophrenic banter that someone should have had the foresight to record. It was a particularly poignant Sunday dinner exchange about my great-grandmother's sister that caused this mental withdrawal of mine at the dining room table.

All I remember from that meal was hearing incomplete phrases yelled out in rapid fire. Actress! This is delicious! Actress? What actress? A lady of the night! Pass the asparagus. No she wasn't! More gravy, anyone? She was a prostitute! Don't you ever say that! Ma, who could afford fur in those days? You need more gravy? I'm telling you! Finish your plate!

At the time I watched it all like a pinball machine, following the conversation as it bounced around the table without order or reason, wondering when it would drop through the flippers. I eventually learned that it never goes through the flippers. It just continues like this until you walk away from the table. So until the dishes are cleared, I simply zone it all out at dinnertime. But right now, I'm lacking the focus necessary to appropriately zone out, so this will just have to be dinner in the raw.

Most of what you need to know about a family can be learned by eating dinner with them. Not in a restaurant, that doesn't count. A dinner in their home. There's something about the combination of food, familiarity, and the comfort of one's home that creates the trifecta for genuine behavior. If a family is thoughtful and warm with each other when they eat together, chances are they act the same when not passing peas. If no one says please or thank you at the table, don't count on them saying it to strangers on the street. And if a person is screaming about gravy while someone else casually slips into conversation that your great-grandmother's sister was a prostitute, well, then that family is probably crazy.

I follow Vanessa to the dining room and find the table set in its traditional fashion. Normally we eat at the island in the kitchen, but on holidays or special days, the dining room table is set formally. A formal setting simply means we drink water out of wine glasses and there are candles on the table. Ten years ago my mother bought two Thanksgiving candles with large wax turkeys sitting at the bottom and somehow we all agreed they were far too nice to light. Since that year, the turkey candles have made an appearance at all our special meals. Although, no one ever comments on how random it is that turkey candles are on the table in spring and that we dim the lights but refuse to light them.

Taking my seat, I give the candles a nod and a smile that says, "Hello, boys. This should be another good one." I comment on the vintage of the Brita water as my grandma places a ten-pound bowl of mashed potatoes in front of me. I'm convinced she believes there is a direct correlation between amount of starch ingested and quality of life. She starts to scoop a big mound onto my plate.

"Uh, Gram, I don't know if I'm in the mashed potato mood right now."

"No? I prepared for that!"

Running to the kitchen and then back to the dining room with an equally large bowl full of roasted potatoes, she gleams with lion-feeding happiness. There's something about a person running and laughing with multiple bowls of potatoes that is unsettling and yet, so reminiscent of home.

"Great. Thanks."

Conversation quickly ensues and that simply means we talk about the meal. At our dinners the meal is the guest of honor and everyone talks about it like it has just cured cancer. But before it cured cancer it traveled the world and discovered the meaning of life. So there are a million questions for the meal even though it's food and can't respond. There's never a lull because there is always something to ask about the food in front of us. What's this called? Where'd you find this recipe? Did you have any trouble getting this beef through security? And it's not just talk about the dinner we're eating, but dinners we've eaten or will eat. I sit quietly amazed that my head doesn't explode when I'm asked for the seventh time if I "remember that meal."

Listening to everyone talk I get the feeling that no one is paying attention to anything anyone is saying. If they were, they might comment on the fact that compliments are being paid to root vegetables or that my father is mentioning again that he'd like to knock down a wall in the dining room to create more of a flow through the house. He mentions this every time we sit together for a meal as if it's a design idea that has just come to him. We've all learned to just ignore it. Grandma is playing event coordinator and only stays seated at the table in three-minute intervals before jumping up to check on a ding, buzz, or beep. Every time she gets up it's a unanimous call for her to relax. Shouting, "Grandma, please sit down" is the only part of the meal we're all on the same page.

I'm pushing my food around hoping everyone will just hurry up and finish so I can go to sleep. When my family takes notice of my full plate, the questioning begins.

"Jess, you haven't touched the roasted potatoes, or the mashed potatoes."

"Or the pork, or turkey, or roast beef."

I stare at the turkey candles and scream at them inside my head. *Who makes twenty pounds of potatoes and three kinds of meat for one meal?! Three kinds of meat! Don't they realize how wrong that is?!*

The interrogation around me continues.

"Is the food cold?"

"Is something too salty?"

"You're not a vegetarian now are you? You need protein!"

"I think they get protein from beans."

"Beans? You call that a meal?"

"Aren't you hungry?"

And there it is. The three most dreaded words to hear at my family's dinner table, particularly when Gram is

17

visiting. For my grandma, "Aren't you hungry?" sets about more panic than, "Are you choking?" Lack of appetite is the inexplicable. If someone isn't breathing, it makes sense that they can't eat. But to have a clear air passage and not want food? Not want potatoes? What the hell is wrong with you?

I look to Vanessa, who's sitting beside me smiling. She has always enjoyed the family giving me a hard time. "Beans, Jess?" she asks with a sardonic look of concern. I bury my head into her shoulder and we both start to laugh. The questions bouncing around the table coupled with the ding buzz beeps coming from the kitchen create the pinball machine that is our dinner hour. With my head hidden in the bobbing motion of my sister's shoulder, it all hits me. Like flashes, the entire day hits me. I'm done with school. I was sitting at graduation and I didn't even realize. I left my great little apartment. I loved that place. I said goodbye to my friends. I don't have a job. My professor was right. What the hell am I doing?

I lift my head to realize I'm crying. Getting up from the table and running to the solace of the cool fresh sheets, I hear my grandmother ask in panic, "Should I have made au gratin?"

In bed, covering my face with a pillow, I pay attention to inhales and exhales hoping to settle down. I'm never so conscious of my breathing as when I'm at home. Breathing in is always met with a thought to do it with patience, and my exhales are always noticeably louder. I just want to lie here, in this room that's not mine, and focus on my breaths until I'm calm. My Aunt Patty was always big into alternative medicines and used to play calming therapeutic tapes in her house. I'd kill for one right now. The soothing voice of the speaker made me fall asleep in minutes. Instructing me to concentrate on my breathing the speaker asked me to relax my eyebrows, my mouth, my shoulders, imagining body parts sinking through the floor with relaxation. I'd wake up so well rested and refreshed, it was wonderful. Years later I learned they were hypnotic weight loss tapes. It helped explain why I used to scream out "No, no, no!" before eating fried foods.

A METAPHORICAL BONNET

Have you ever stopped to watch people in an electronics store near the video cameras? I love those displays where they'll hook a camera up to a large television and record people passing by. Have you ever stopped to watch that? Everyone seems to have the same reaction. A person walks by the TV, does a double take when he spots himself, and then repositions his body so that he can watch his own wave in High Definition. Everyone uses that same hesitant wave in order to fully establish that they're looking at their own image. The wave interests me. It's surprising to find yourself where you don't expect to be found, like on a giant screen at Best Buy. But even after stopping to look, and recognizing the setup, it's fascinating that we're all still inclined to move our hand slowly in front of our face, just to be sure. Then, after a few moments, after fully establishing that, yup, that's me, we move on.

Moving back home without an idea of where I'll be moving next feels a bit like being that unassuming shopper browsing through electronics. I've spent this first week at home just looking around, not really thinking of my place, until the randomness of my family puts it on a big screen right in front of my face. If something seems familiar, I linger the way I would with a wave for the camera until finally realizing, oh, I'm home.

Growing up on a farm instills permanence in the idea of home. Home isn't an ever-changing place because so much of farming revolves around routine and predictability. I've always been able to use home as a point of reference because it always stays the same. We live within apple orchards and endless fields of cabbage and squash, but any idea that you might have about a farm—propaganda pumped out by the wonderful people at Country Time Lemonade—does not apply to our house. It smells like coleslaw and freshly mowed grass, and my father wouldn't have it any other way. He believes lawn care is the measure of a man. Our "farm dogs" are a Pomeranian named Gizmo and a Maltese named Bubbles, who bark constantly at nothing and escape daily to the fields behind our house, forcing us to chase after them with a treat yelling, "Cheese!" And yet, it's always this great mystery as to where all the cheddar has gone.

Save for the roar of tractors and machinery, it's relatively quiet. But my parents decided long ago to combat that silence with the sound of their own voices. So just when you've settled in for a relaxing nap or plopped down with a good book, enjoying the warm breeze blowing through the open windows, my father will come running in, causing the dogs to go crazy, asking for someone to come mow the lawn, followed by my mother yelling from the garage for help with the groceries.

My mother comes from a long line of shouters. I grew up thinking the volume was for the benefit of the older folks, so that they might hear the conversations, but that wasn't the case at all. Everyone just liked to shout. George Costanza's parents remind me of about half of my relatives.

The irony of our chaotic farmhouse serves as a constant source of confusion for me. Despite the rural surroundings, my family has been able to create all the noise and commotion of Grand Central within our home. Something is always lost and there is a loud, frantic search to find it. Keys! My wallet! The phone bill! Any day of the week could give way to a bizarre reality game show in which we hunt through the contents of a room for something that is most likely in my mother's pocketbook. And instead of simply walking to another room to see if someone is there, my parents use the country intercom that is their own holler.

I used to tell myself that they were partially deaf and needed to yell. But I later realized they were simply trying to kill me with their own voices. I'm incredibly sensitive to sound—ringing phones, loud chewers, the clicking noise a car blinker makes—and the sound of my parents' raised voices is enough to drive me insane. I remember seeing footage of the standoff at Waco, Texas and how the police used loud soundtracks of annoying sounds to drive the people out of the compound. All it would have taken for me to leave was 35 seconds of my mother talking into the microphone. "Jess, the dogs are running away! Bring the cheese!"

Being at home is like waiting for the boom that follows the burst of color from a firework. For the most part it's enjoyable, but at any given moment you know an explosion of sound will be coming. So even when you're alone, your shoulders are raised just slightly to your ears and your eyes squint just a tad, because a few hours from now, someone will be yelling at the top of their lungs that we've lost Bubbles.

For as much as I know about this place, I'm starting to feel like a refugee in my own house. All of my belongings are packed and I intend to keep them that way because to unpack would mean I'm staying, and I refuse to believe that. I'm just taking a minute to catch my breath and then I'll be moving on. Although, feeling temporary in a place so fixed in my mind, using home as a pit-stop or a train depot or something, is making me feel weird. As soon as home becomes a place to visit, an unspoken disruption occurs. Returning to a place that at one time held everything

I knew about the world, and to see how small that was, creates an awkward elitism. I've moved on, but the house has remained. It welcomes me back with open doors reminding me of who I was and where I came from but I try to act aloof like those things are so passé. I'm trying to live in the now while this house and my parents would prefer to think I'm still seven. It always confused me that my grandma would make my mom sandwiches and bring them to her on a snack tray when we visited, but now I get it.

My father woke me up yesterday at 4:30 in the morning with a glass of orange juice saying, "Jess, sit up and have a swig of OJ. It's a great way to start the day."

I sat up reluctantly with sleeping limbs, thinking, *My day isn't going to start for about another eight hours, why am I drinking this juice?* And then I remembered.

On family vacations we used to stay at chain hotels that offered free continental breakfasts because my parents have a severe weakness for complimentary breakfast pastry. With an internal farm alarm, my dad would always wake up much earlier and hit the breakfast before us, bringing back juice as an amuse bouche. Realizing that we sort of loved this on our trips, he held on to the idea with a militant loyalty, waking us up "for a swig of juice" nearly every morning. Somehow, when not in Orlando, particularly at 4:30 in the morning, the simple charm behind this tradition escaped me.

For children, home exists as a living museum of Remember When. Coming home after college is a lot like visiting Colonial Williamsburg and being forced to join in with the role-play. Except at home the plaques read, "This is how we used to wake you up for school," instead of, "This is how the settlers made and preserved jam." You are the audience in the tours through The Way Things Used To Be, with your parents playing the guides who keep insisting that you speak in Olde English.

All you want to do is say, "Don't you see? We've

moved on!" But there's something sort of sweet about it so you play along until you realize you've become one of those tourists who takes pictures in the stocks and buys a pilgrim hat or bonnet at the gift shop and you think, where the hell am I going to wear this bonnet? The bonnet is a metaphor.

Maybe I went too far. I'm not sure what the bonnet stands for. But the guides have been more than generous, and you just don't have the strength to ask them to stop. So you try to exist there, knowing who you are now has no place in this land of once was. No one wants to live in Colonial Williamsburg. It's depressing.

I imagine the Amish can relate to this—still with the horse and buggy after all these years. You have to know that at some point an Amish couple has been late for an important engagement and as the cars zip by one after another, they look to the horse, and then back at each other and say, "Now this is just silly."

I tried explaining all of this to my parents the other night. I talked about home as a museum, the bonnet, and the symbol of the electronic store display. I went into the whole thing about catching myself off guard on a big screen, surprised to see myself where I didn't think I'd be found, and they both looked at me like I was crazy. Granted, it didn't make loads of sense, but the conversation ended with my dad urging me to research a few televisions before buying one. I'd forgotten that being at home means that at almost no point will I be understood. I think that's a general rule that most people can relate to, but it seems to apply to middle children more than anyone.

Besides the obvious—lack of baby pictures, mind blanks on your name during introductions—you become aware very early of what it means to be a middle child.

For me, it came every Easter when we would search for baskets. We never did the egg thing, it was always a basket hunt, and mine was always in the oven. My sisters would search everywhere, my mom often rearranging furniture to hide theirs. I always walked directly to the oven and pulled it out.

"Oh, Vicki, you found it!"

"It's Jessica."

But if there are two universals about kids it's that they love to be timed—with anything—and they love to look for shit. So the idea of a hunt for gifts carried over to all our birthdays. Our presents would be hidden in various places around the house to add to the fun. It was exciting to run around hunting for glimpses of wrapping paper, until it ceased to be, and we'd cry. Realizing the whole house was too daunting, and all we really wanted was our stuff, the hiding places were narrowed down to two rooms: the living room and the kitchen. I think the kitchen was included solely for the purposes of my gifts.

This tradition continued as we grew up and the hiding spots could be listed with about as much effort as reciting the alphabet. It lasted through the eye-rolling angst of the preteens, "Oh, under the sofa cushion?! Good one mom—God!" Through the high school, "No, I'm too old for that. But, ok, hide them. No, really. Hide them." And I tried to carry it to college but the girls on my floor freshman year weren't feeling it.

"Have you seen my paper?"

"HAPPY BIRTHDAY!"

"No, seriously. I'm late for class and this is a huge deal."

"Then you better get to looking! Cold, colder."

"Idiot."

Returning home is to be reminded daily that if we were to hide gifts right at this moment, mine would be in the oven. Even though Sabrina is off living her life and I've been gone for years, a week at home has slipped me right back into Middle Child Syndrome.

If unfamiliar, MCS is a highly common but rarely discussed condition that affects millions of kids growing up and continues to haunt them throughout early adulthood. It can be complex to describe to those who have no personal knowledge of the topic but it basically works as such:

1) Parents have first child.

—This is new and exciting.

—Pictures are taken.

—Everything the child does is adorable. Examples: "Oh, look, it ate something!" "Oh look, it spit out that thing it just ate!"

—Parents subconsciously or not, place all their hopes in dreams in this child.

2) Parents have second child.

—The first uses of "Been there done that" are said to have come when early man and woman had their second child. I think William Safire wrote a column about it.

3) Parents have last child.

—This is final and exciting.

—Pictures are taken.

—Everything the child does is adorable and memorable because it's the last time around.

—Subconsciously or not, the parents will give this child anything she wants.

Middle children are almost born with an intrinsic knowledge of this series of events. If you're an only child, it's a mix of everything. If you're one of two, you're probably healthier than you think. If you come from more than five, you probably just think that being ignored is how children are raised. But my primary concern is with the middle of three. They are born knowing their place. Even though the third has yet to arrive, they know. As a result, the child's position in life is centered on observation.

Observation is key to the existence of the middle child and paramount to overcoming MCS because for the most part, members of their own family tend not to hear them when they speak. "Sorry, did you say something?" is the number one question asked to middle children. I'm sure at some point in history a middle child said something really beautiful or made a poignant statement about the human condition. Unfortunately, no one was listening so that's a loss for the masses. Middle children know, and friends of middle children soon learn, that the majority of things they say are under their breath and mumbled, because they're already preconditioned for no one to hear. It's not sad it's just true.

My cousins who are middle siblings and I have a meeting once a year to discuss varying degrees of MCS. At Christmas a few years ago, my cousin Karianne told this story:

While looking through her family's safety deposit box for her birth certificate, she came across an envelope that read, "Steven's Teeth." Steven is her older brother and the envelope contained all of his baby teeth. Digging through more of the box, she found an envelope that read, "Julia's Teeth." Julia is her younger sister. Searching the safe in its entirety she was unable to find an envelope with her name on it. That night at dinner, she shouted out in protest, "Where are my teeth?!"

Her story sufficiently sums up the fundamental middle child experience. Where are my teeth, indeed. It all falls under the series of events of birth order: First child looses his teeth, it's new and exciting. Last child looses her teeth, it's final and memorable. Middle child looses her teeth and well, how many envelopes of teeth do we really need?

Attempting to talk to my parents or sisters about my situation, namely that I haven't a fucking clue what I should do with my life, has proven to be incredibly difficult. Vanessa is in the last moments of her senior year in high school and just thinking about what that was like is annoying so I'm not even going to attempt to ask her for her advice. I called Sabrina a week ago to see if she had any suggestions, and before I could get my hello in she started talking about feng shui and how she was trying to find which animal she was to determine the feng shui that best suited her. "I thought I was a monkey but it turns out I'm a goat. And let me tell you, I am totally a goat." After listening to her go on for an hour about her goals to become a barn animal in the name of home décor, I hung up. Middle children often end up talking to themselves, if only because it ensures someone will be listening.

My parents have always been more than willing to hear, but hearing is a distant relative to listening. The day following my mini-breakdown at the dining room table, after crying and running away from my full plate, my mom commented on the spectacle and said it was OK if I was a vegetarian. It was a nice thought but she was totally missing the source of my distress. I could have told her I was overcome by graduation, scared by my lack of plans, and not thrilled to be home, but I figured I'd just let her think that I don't like meat.

This is a common disconnect between parent and child; the attempts to help, the desire to be helped, and the complete inability to understand each other. Have you ever been lost in a foreign country where you didn't speak a word of the native language? That's exactly what parent/ child communication is, only with fewer exaggerated arm movements.

So, using the reliable MCS observation skills of yore, I've resigned myself to picking up on the ridiculous nature of my time here at home. I'm a shopper in electronics, caught off guard, baffled by a familiar image on a 54-inch plasma. I'm talking to myself, trying to figure out the answers on my own, all the while waving at a confused girl who looks just like me. I'm living in the Remember When Museum, trying to establish who I'm going to be in the future. And presently, I'm more inclined to check inside the oven before heating it up, just in case someone has thought to surprise me with a gift.

LIFE GOAL LISTS AND SOMEONE ELSE'S T-SHIRT

With my morning juice in the darkness of the night and Nessa getting ready for school around 6:30, sleeping in is never even close to an option. But by 7:30 the house is mine and I decide to take advantage of the quiet.

I use my alone time in the morning to stand in front of the bathroom mirror and stare at my face. I hope to inspire myself to come up with a concrete plan for the day by using a long expressionless stare at my own reflection. It usually doesn't work. After that, I greet myself using different accents. My British, Scottish, and French accents are on fire. My Australian could use some work. Then I go to the living room where I do three sit-ups before turning on the TV to channel surf and try to catch a *Frasier* rerun. *Frasier* was a brilliant show. If one were to write down and research every unknown word, artist, or reference mentioned in that show, it might be an appropriate substitution for an undergraduate education. Note to self: Look up Renata Tebaldi.

These have been a difficult few weeks. I imagine the planners of the first Thanksgiving Day Parade went through something similar to what I'm experiencing now. The parade was over and then suddenly thoughts of, "Oh shit. What should we do with all these floats?" I'm just digesting the fact that I'm done with school and trying to relax about it. To their credit, my parents have been wonderful. A few comments have been made about my wardrobe choices, but that's only natural. I've had a lifetime of my mother's condescending remarks about my clothes.

Once before a wedding, my sisters put on their dresses while my mother kept saying, "That's an attention-getter! What an attention-getter!" Up until about the sixth grade, an item of clothing was never considered for purchase unless there was a strong possibility it would help me glow in the dark. Because I spent most of my formative years wearing fluorescent clothes, taking all of my fashion cues from highlighters, I've had my fill of attention-getters. So hearing her repeat the phrase "attention-getter" really upset me. I remember when she asked me to get dressed I dryly responded, "I'm just going to wear what I have on and then set myself on fire when we get there. That should turn a few heads."

Since I've been home, I've had to justify my clothing choices daily. Like when my mom came home from work the other day:

"Still in your pj's, Jess?"

"No, I changed."

"Oh." she said. Biting her upper lip and nodding slowly.

I like to buy my t-shirts at the Salvation Army and thrift stores, and I wear t-shirts just about all of the time. For some reason it drives my mother crazy. She's constantly asking me why I want to wear someone else's shirt. But other than the occasional "Your clothes look like pajamas" comments, I've been free just to be. I've had some time to think about things, but I've wasted most of that time. A lot of kids take time to travel after graduation to clear their heads. I've been napping.

It's daunting to assess your situation after college, particularly for someone like me who has never been good with decisions. As a child I would often be overwhelmed by menus in restaurants and instead chose to order nothing. It was my own little hunger strike to protest free will at Red Lobster. During those self-starvations my family's adage of "You can never go wrong with grilled cheese" was born, and continues to ring true to this day. But with questions of life direction, forget about it. I'm seven-years-old again with a billboard for a menu.

The difficulty in saying what I want lies in the fear of never having it, or the fear of having it but not liking it. I bet that's true for a lot of people. Building excitement around an idea only to have it fade awkwardly away probably plays a big part in not voicing our hopes and goals. It reminds me of college basketball games when the cameras from ESPN film the student section, causing everyone to scream and stick up their index fingers. I often wondered what would happen if the camera stayed on one student for two minutes. For five minutes? An entire half? Would they continue to scream? At what point do they think, OK, maybe I should stop screaming now? I don't know if we should ever enter into anything without that excitement, but what if we can't keep it up? We're a society obsessed with success and the first to ridicule those who find it. Thus, we try not to shout out what we really want so as to avoid anyone hearing it and holding us to it.

Kierkegaard said, "There is nothing with which everyman is so afraid as getting to know how enormously much he is capable of doing and becoming." I think he had a point there, and it might help explain why I just keep loafing around the house. But enough is enough. It's time for a game plan, a call to action. I have to figure out what I'm doing and do it. I'll just sit here with a pen and some paper and brainstorm. A good ol' fashioned think tank of one. I'm not going to edit myself because that's how the fear of what's possible enters. I'll simply jot down a rapid-fire list of life goals, stream of consciousness style.

The last time I made a list of goals was in the fourth grade and among the things I wanted to do was see a Paula Abdul concert. In retrospect, it wasn't so horrible that I missed out on achieving that one.

OK. Question 1:

Who do you want to be? As a person?

Whoa there, Harpo Studios! Hold up a minute. Couldn't have started with interests? OK, fair enough, we'll start big. Who do I want to be? *Who the hell am I?* might be the more appropriate question. I've had my whole life to get to know me and I'm still a little confused as to what I'm all about. I wonder if I read a description of myself I'd even notice it was me. I don't even wear my own shirts.

It's hard to figure out who I want to become because I don't have that memory of strongly affirming what I wanted to be when I grew up. I know at one point when I was five or six, I desperately wanted to be McGuyver, but I don't think that counts. I even went so far as to get the haircut.

It was the first time my mom allowed me to go back to the stylist's chair alone while she waited up front, and I took full advantage of her absence. It was this little salon where the hairstylists went by horse names, instead of using their real names. This is never a good sign. When fake names are used in business, you have to assume it's so that you can't find that person's home number in the phonebook. But I was perfectly willing to ask a woman named Gumdrops for the "McGuyver." I described the mullet-like cut I was going for and asked her to keep some length for a tail. If my parents didn't know I was gay back then, I don't know what other signs would have tipped them off. When I met my mom at the front of the salon, she burst into tears. I remember her crying up until she cut off my tail while I was in the bathtub. I think that's why I don't like baths. But I digress.

I guess when I think of a person I admire or would hope to become I do have a picture in mind. To be that carefree girl who plays guitar and always wins on those instant lotto scratch cards or those claw-machine games and gives the prizes to little kids, because a simple sort of luck follows her. And wherever she goes she gives people genuine thrilled-to-see-you smiles and they ask the waitress to send over a glass of milk with her meal, on them, because they know that's what she likes. And when she leaves, hands in back pockets, head tilted up, people comment on her spirit.

I'm not this girl. I'm the girl who steps in gum. And when I walk away, dragging my right foot, I can actually hear the impression I've made on others. "Oh, watch out. That girl stepped in something."

I stop and review what I have written. I aspire to be someone who drinks milk with meals and is good at the claw game. Well, that's a cover letter right there.

Shit.

Question 2:

What do you want to do? As a career?

Staring at the question, I roll my eyes at my timing. Yeah, maybe should have thought about that during college, genius.

I majored in film, which seemed very natural for me. I liked to watch movies, why not spend a few years exploring why? However, student films quickly erase the allure of filmmaking. Huge sweeping ideas or tragic horrible deaths are squeezed into ten-minute shorts that we expect people to take seriously. "Yeah, I just met that girl seven minutes ago, I really don't care that she's dead."

Between the horrible acting of the kid down the hall, whom you begged to star in it, and the lame effects you use on Avid or Final Cut Pro, you're left with something not so great that's costing you around $33,000 a year. But someone in your class will say that the clichés and weak acting were used as commentary on the student film in general. It's so bad it's funny. So funny it's true, so true it's sad, so sad it resonates. You're given a B and told to stop using so many fade-ins.

I think about it and decided that a career path in mockumentaries seems most appropriate for me. It's like the documentary, only without all the research, and that sounds like a boat I could sail. I put a little star by mockumentary and lightly punch my left arm. Attagirl, Jess, you set a goal.

Question 3:

Where do you want to be?

I'll take "Anywhere But Here" for $500, Alex.

Don't get me wrong, my parents have been fantastic about allowing me this breathing time to figure out where I'm headed. But slowly slipping into the worst version of myself is hard to do in front of mom and dad. I'm an extension of them so when the biggest part of my day is *The Price is Right*, they don't have to say it, but I know they're not thrilled. And parents already have a raw deal as it is. In college I found myself, on multiple occasions, bitching at my mother about various trivial things during her weekly call. I'd mention these complaints to no one but her for the sole reason that she was my mom, and thus by default, must care. They raised me and my sisters to be kind, thoughtful people, essentially to everyone except them. I'm aware of this short stick and wish them no extra grief. That's part of the reason I stopped myself the other day from going into detail about why I think *The Price Is Right* is a metaphor for life. I'll spare you as well, but it basically breaks down to being able to guess the actual retail price of your soul. It was a complex allegory. It made sense in my head.

But the morning game show has become a staple of my daily life, and somewhere on this goal list I have to take steps to change that. When you start to become upset at the prizes that are given away, you know it's time to evaluate your life. For instance, I'm constantly amazed by how many grandfather clocks are used as prizes. Most of the contestants are in L.A. on vacation, so even if they were to win a grandfather clock—which in my opinion is the lamest prize ever—it would cost them nearly $500 to ship it home to Oklahoma. In which case, why not just buy a grandfather clock in Oklahoma? I spend an hour each morning yelling at the television over stupid prizes like dinette sets, or new carpets, or pop-up trailers. About 98% of the audience is either in college, in the military, or elderly. Where the hell are they going to put a pop-up trailer?

I always thought if I ever wrote a movie I would have a supporting character, maybe the friend of the main character, become addicted to *The Price Is Right* and have him hang out at grocery stores memorizing prices of various products. I realize I've become that supporting character and that depresses me beyond description.

OK, stream of consciousness is not helpful when making lists. Under Question 3 I've scribbled "Showcase Showdown" over and over.

Questions 4-7 deal with family, relationships, financial goals and positive impacts I'd like to make on the world, but I don't think I can honestly answer any of those questions before putting on pants. Success experts suggest starting with larger goals and then working down to more immediate ones, but the pants thing seems pretty important. It's hard to make a list of goals when the biggest thing I've done in the last few weeks is finish viewing my family's entire video library, minus *Speed*, which I vowed never to watch again after I found myself quoting Keanu Reeves on an all too regular basis. "Cans! They're just cans!"

I take a break from the list to get dressed for the day, but stepping away from the sheet of paper only makes me think about it more. Can lifetime achievements be checked off like daily tasks? Do these lists actually work for people? I know they've never really worked for me. I've always just viewed items on a list as things that can be put off until later. The most pressing issues are never put on lists, they're just things you know you have to do. You'll never see a list that looks like this:

1) Make hand stop bleeding
2) Find finger
3) Go to the hospital to see if they can reattach finger
4) Buy stamps

Knowing what you need to do doesn't require a list. But not knowing what you need to do makes for a completely incoherent list, so why am I even worrying about it anyway? If I made an honest list of things to do, I'm pretty sure I would just feel worse.

1) Change underwear
2) Leave the house
3) Work on Australian accent
4) Watch *Speed*. You know you want to.

Grabbing a fresh t-shirt and a pair of jeans out of my bag, I hear my dad come into the house. Everyday around noon, he comes over from the farm for lunch and finds me lounging in the living room. In an attempt to get me off the sofa he usually asks, with a motivational tone, if I'd care to join him. Even though noon is more like my breakfast hour, I always get up and take a seat at the island in the kitchen, if only to watch him make his meal.

My father has a fantastically loud lunch preparation routine; it's a dance really. Starting at the fridge he unloads any possible item he thinks he'll want to eat, frequently singing to himself and shifting his weight from one foot to another. "Hey, are we out of cheese again?" he'll ask, in between verses of a song about lunch he's making up on the spot. Bouncing over to the cabinets, he'll grab plates and cup, and then spin to the drawers, fumbling with silverware before sliding to the pantry for pretzels or chips, rustling the bags more than necessary because I think he just likes the noise. Opening pickle jars, slicing bread, everything seems to have a heightened sound effect when he does it. And he is the king of the oversized sandwich. I'm not exactly sure how he manages to eat them but it is success every time.

While he enjoys lunch entirely, he has a slightly insane obsession with expiration dates. He thinks one of the big ways he helps out around the house is by eating left-overs and questionable deli meat. Whenever my mom starts to complain about work needing to be done he'll chime in with, "Well, who ate that eggplant parmesan that was going to go bad?" And it's always halfway through his lunch that he realizes he should have eaten something else.

"Shoot, we still have that ham in there, don't we?"

"You know, I'm not really sure," I reply.

He moves slowly to the refrigerator, afraid of what he knows he'll find.

"I knew it! Darn! Will you eat that up for lunch?"

"No, I won't be doing that."

"Fine, let it go bad. I'll eat it tomorrow."

That's a classic martyr move for him. My dad needs to be seen as the one who is forever sacrificing: eating old food, working long hours, insisting that he could live in sub-zero conditions. If my father were to give a lecture on gain-ing control of your life, he would spend three hours talking about the importance of the thermostat. During winter that tiny box on the wall becomes his main reason for living. He really believes that he gains some sort of moral superiority with each degree he knocks off of the room temperature. If a foreign exchange student had ever lived with us, their first fluent sentence would have been, "Put on another sweater."

I sit there as he eats, seeing that he is now visibly up-set to be enjoying fresh cold cuts, and I try not to comment on the chewing noises he makes. As previously mentioned, I'm very sensitive to this sound and my father's heightened sound effects carry over to his chewing. So sitting in an oth-erwise silent house listening to him eat a sandwich is my own personal hell.

"So tell me about your day" (chew chew chew.)

"I just got up, Dad. Not much to tell." (Please stop chewing.)

"I'm glad you took some time off. I think you just

37

needed to rest." (Noisy gulp.)

"Yeah." (Really, stop.)

"Your uncles were asking me what kind of job you want to get. I said Film Editing. That's what you want to do, right?"

"Um, yeah." (Noisy gulp). "Or production, I'm not really sure. I was actually just making a list of possible--"

"It's exciting Jess!" he said, interrupting me. "The movies! Do you think it would help if you said Steve Martin is your dad?" This asked with a big smile as he elbows my arm.

My dad has great pride in his name, thanks to the comic success of "the other Steve Martin," as he refers to him. Whenever he leaves his name for dinner reservations he waits anxiously for the hostess's response. Grinning widely he'll say, "Nope, not that one!" And it's impossible to watch *Father of the Bride* or *The Jerk* without hearing, "Oh, boy. This should be good!" when his name comes up in the opening titles.

Staring at his cartoon-like sandwich, quite certain that he can't hear me over his own chewing, I mumble, "I don't know dad, it might."

Digging through a bag of carrot sticks he continues. "I can make a few calls, tell a few jokes. I mean, who doesn't love Steve Martin?"

I'm pretty sure he'd keep this conversation going with or without a response from me, but I offer an apathetic "OK, great."

"But you can stay here for as long as you want while you look for jobs, you know that."

"Thanks, I know."

"Just so you know there's no rush." Looking at my t-shirt and taking another bite of his sandwich he says, "Palma Sola Panthers? Whose shirt is that?" (Chew chew chew.)

There is so definitely a rush.

PERHAPS A CHICKEN PLACE

I'm having trouble finding a job. No wait, that's not phrased correctly. I'm finding numerous jobs. I'm applying to an insane amount of jobs. I'm having almost no trouble finding jobs. The difficulty lies in actually getting one.

I must have been absent on the day "What To Do When Your Plans Fall Through" was taught at school because I'm currently at a loss. I distinctly remember learning the "Study hard, get good grades" lesson back in Junior High. That's the lesson on which all my plans were based. I trusted that working hard in school would make easy work of finding a job. Oh, cruel train of naiveté! You carried me as a passenger all those years, before dumping me off at Graduation Junction with a boarding pass for Reality Express.

My plan didn't account for needing more than a balanced base of book learning. The plan was to bulk up my GPA to compensate for my lack of actual experience and I thought that some good old fashioned A's would land me a nice little career somewhere (Choo Choo!).

It seems the entire nation of graduating seniors got the memo about good grades. I don't regret for a second spending time and energy on learning, but as far as Honors and Dean's Lists go, they're all expired warranties on the job hunt. Everyone I went to school with was smart and talented. How am I supposed to jump out to employers? Accepting applicants for a job interview must be like judging a beauty pageant. "Gosh, they all sort of look the same. But this one plays the harp and started a non-profit water polo program in Guam, so we're going to go with her."

When you're looking for any type of entry-level job, it's important to highlight that you can do the following:

—Make copies

—Use Excel

—Answer the phone

The footnote to these abilities is that you must demonstrate to a prospective employer that you have professional experience doing all of the above. I've been answering the phone since I was a little kid, but because I was never paid to do so in a professional setting, it doesn't count. And if we're being honest, I'm not entirely sure I know how to use Excel. Shit.

Employers love to stress the experience thing, which I would so gladly have, if someone would give me a job. I was too busy during my summers in college trying to make money for college that I never had time to intern. So let's take a look at my work experience, shall we? The summer before my freshman year in college I worked as a janitor at an elementary school. But I can't put "Janitor" on my résumé so I play around with different titles including General Maintenance Technician, Custodial Aide, and Portier, which I think is just French for janitor. I eventually decide to omit it from my job experience category altogether.

The summer after my freshman year of college I worked as a housekeeper at a lodge in Alaska. This one is hard to spin for two reasons. First, it sounds made up. And if anyone ever does call me for an interview, I'm not sure how I'd explain it.

"So, Rooms Division Satisfaction Monitor? What

was that exactly?"

"Um, housekeeper."

"In Alaska?"

"Right. Well, cleaning toilets and handling the soiled sheets of complete strangers in the Lower 48 just lacked a certain amount of adventure. I was drawn to the opportunity to vacuum guests' rooms with the imminent threat of a bear attack."

I worked two full-time summer jobs before studying in London in order to have enough beer money for a semester abroad. One job was at a state park checking in campers, which left me smelling like a campfire every night. The other was as a baker at a local bagel shop, which required that I arrive at 4:00 AM, bake bagels non-stop for eight hours, and work in a room that was never less than 110 degrees thanks to a giant oven and a huge vat of boiling water. You can imagine how well the oven/steam/freak pituitary gland combo went over. My baking uniform was an XXL t-shirt because my 18-year-old boss refused to order me a different size, and a pair of black pants that I was supposed to supply. But I was working two crappy jobs to make money, not spend it, so instead of buying new black pants, I used an old pair of black Lycra pants. I showed up to work everyday wearing an XXL t-shirt tucked into Lycra—creating all sorts of excess material bulge—and a visor. I figured baking was a behind the scenes gig, so I didn't care. However, the baking room had a giant window as a wall so that customers could watch the baking process while waiting to order. Thus, the baker and her ridiculous outfit became part of the show. Sweating profusely from the early morning until noon and swearing like a motherfucker every time I burnt myself, the baking job was really more of a performance art piece than a summer job. I eventually had my little sister call and quit for me.

I've also omitted Bagel Baker from my work experience history.

So the résumé I've been sending out to employers includes this impressive list of credentials: Film degree with no actual film experience, Park Aide, and Alaskan House-keeper.

Add to all of this the pressure of finding a *dream job*. In the same way that adults should never wear footie-pajamas, college graduates should never take jobs unrelated to their dreams. At least that's the vibe I'm getting from all these people who keep asking me about my dream job, like it's something that exists and is waiting for me. It's no longer enough to have a job, now it should be the job of my dreams. Which is what, exactly? I have no idea. I'm never working in my dreams. In my dreams I'm made of Fluff and can eat my own face. I'll just take a regular job, thanks.

After weeks of waking up with no classes to attend or job to show up to, you become aware of the importance of these things in that they give you something to do. My older sister Sabrina took a more proactive approach to the job hunt and had gainful employment established for herself upon graduation. I guess a lot of people do this. I'm begin-ning to think they might be on to something.

I called her the other day to talk to her about my situation and share with her the anxiety attack I had a few mornings ago. It was Saturday and when I rolled over and looked at the alarm clock it said 7:00 AM. Jumping out of bed, screaming that I was late for work, I frantically searched for clothes. Vanessa got up (I'm still sharing her room) and asked me to stop. I looked around and realized, phew, I'm not late! It's ok, it's Saturday. I'm not late. Followed by the realization that I don't have a job for which I could be late. Followed by intense chest pains, and I went back to sleep.

I was relaying the irony behind this to Brina as we spoke.

"Bri, I'm jumping up in the early morning to cel-ebrate the fact that I'm not late for a job I don't have."

"You're thinking about it too much. Just relax and

enjoy this time off."

Her final advice was to keep applying for jobs and something about how only boring people get bored—which didn't serve as much comfort as I sat on the sofa thinking of names for bands. *What's a better name for a band?* has become my new favorite game. I dare say that even at the height of its ingenious flip-face glory, *Guess Who?* lacked the verve of such an exciting Q&A exchange. Although, No, my person is not Bernard (NMPINB) would be a tight name for a band.

Last week I played *What's a better rap name?* and shared the results with my parents at dinner. "Right, so Mom, your rap name is going to be Lil' Debbie Snack Cakes. Dad, you're Cabbage Patch Kid. And I'll be spinning on the ones and twos as DJ Tanner. Oh Mylanta! Get it? But maybe for certain jams I'll have different names because I'm also liking the idea of being called Baby Bok Choy." They both looked at me with concern without saying a word. I was amused at least.

But that was last week and this week it's band names. I begin.

What's a better name for a band?

Shampoo Mohawks OR Des Moines.

Des Moines.

Can You Say Adobe? OR Flat Line Clear.

Can You Say Adobe?

Theo Huxtable OR The Eaten Eyes of Mr. Conehead.

I have to go with Theo Huxtable.

If Friendly's opened in France would it be called le Monsieur Conehead sundae?

I like to think so.

When I start to ask myself questions like this, which are unrelated to the band names, I know I've gone too far and need to stop. But with literally no obligations, I'm not sure what to do with myself. Even if people hate their jobs, it still gives them something to do for eight hours a day, or longer if they do something important. My days consist of early morning cereal, sitting with my father as he eats his lunch, reading a book and walking from room to room. If this sounds sad and pathetic, that's because it is.

Unemployment is an exercise in absolute boredom. It moves beyond channel surfing or dancing in front of the mirror. It is light years away from a lack of things to do. You actually run out of things to think about. Having the house to myself for the mornings, I run through random thoughts until I've exhausted them all.

I saw a show about a self-defense course and was struck by how much was involved. With all the moves and the kicking and shouting and that guy in the weird costume, it just seemed like a lot to remember. I've often thought that the best self-defense can be learned from a precocious child in a technique known as Dead Weight. Often seen in grocery store candy aisles or the toy department of your local Whatever-Mart, said technique is usually employed when a parent or guardian wants the child to move but the child would prefer not to. The entire thing plays out as such: A parent asks the child to follow them, the child refuses, the parent takes their hand making a move for the exit, and the child collapses. The technique gains the attention of bystanders initially because it is odd to see someone sprawled on the floor of a public space, and if executed correctly, can quickly draw a crowd. Most children already know intrinsically to keep their eyes closed during this process in that it gives the illusion of death. As people start to notice the child laying on the ground, the parent becomes embarrassed and tries to lift their child like a sack of potatoes only to have them flop about like a boiled noodle. Exerting the effort to lift a thirty-pound kid to his lifeless feet while explaining to complete strangers that he's not dead, he just wants a Blow-Pop, is difficult.

I sat on the sofa trying to think about how I could

mold this into a training course. I liked the idea of people paying $25 a lesson to show up in spandex and fall to the ground for an hour. I couldn't think of a way to properly execute that so I started to think about the origin of finger quotes people use during conversations to highlight something they're saying. I thought of Chris Farley's brilliant use of finger quotes in his Saturday Night Live sketch and proceeded to imitate him around the house for the rest of the day.

—What did you do today, Jess?

—"Nothing." I don't really "do anything."

Not appreciating where I was coming from, my mom simply said, "OK" with finger quotes like she had caught on to how the game was played.

—Have you "eaten yet" or do you want some "dinner?"

—Dinner would be "good."

All of this random daydreaming and time wasting is merely used to fill gaps in the day for the time spent away from the computer searching for jobs. I use the various job search engines to send out cover letters and résumés by the truckload daily. I can only assume that everyone else is doing the same because I have yet to hear back from a single employer. As a result, I've taken to applying to anything, anywhere, just to see if there's a remote possibility a girl with a degree in TV, Radio, and Film will ever be employed. So many résumés have been sent that if I ever did get a call from a potential employer, I'd have no idea which job they were calling about or from where in the country they were calling. If there's an airport nearby, I've probably looked for a job there. Travel and moving are not the problem. Well, in the immediate future, actually moving from the living room might take some coaxing, but if I were offered a job, I'd be gone by morning.

Not hearing back from any postings in the film industry, I've taken to applying for jobs completely unrelated to anything I know how to do—like a barber or a gymnastics coach.

> To Whom It May Concern:
> While I have no experience cutting hair, I've worked with people and scissors independently of each other in the past. If given the opportunity to combine the two, I think the results could be fantastic (sams).

> Or:

> Dear Potential Employer:
> While I have no experience in gymnast training, I've watched the Summer Olympics since I can remember. I have some great ideas for the floor exercise including running from corner to corner as fast as you can, without actually tumbling or flipping in any way. I don't believe this has ever been done and it might pick up some heavy style points. Or perhaps introduce pair floor exercise routines in which the two gymnasts perform the old classics like wheelbarrow, or the crab walk. I look forward to hearing from you.

Doing this offers a chuckle, and in this process a good chuckle is needed. It's either laugh or allow your morale to wear so thin you'll begin to think Corn Pop consumption is the only talent worth mentioning in the Special Skills section of your résumé.

I'm beginning to view the film major/philosophy minor as one of those cosmic jokes, like the scrotum. And I think college advisors who would have you believe studying these two things is a solid plan for your future should be fired. And their jobs should be given to film/philosophy majors because those people will never get a job anywhere else.

If all else fails maybe I'll just become a country music songwriter; it seems simple enough. The idea is to take large life themes like love or loss or hope and link them to everyday appliances or things lying around the house. People love songs about things. This is the chorus of what is sure to be a hit song, called "Potato Peeler."

Love is a washer/dryer.

Fear is a dried up field.

Missing you is a potato peeler but the taters done been peeled.

I have to work on a few more verses but essentially it's going to end up being about unrequited love and potato skins.

Other hits include, "Wishing I had Amnesia So I'd Forget How Much I Need 'Ya" and "Found An Actor Who Looks Like You, Gonna Go Rent Everything You Do." I have to work on the titles. Maybe they're too long.

To my parents' credit, they've stopped asking me if I've heard back from anywhere. Instead, all questions are posed as, "Where did you apply today?" It gives me a sense of accomplishment by having sent something out, without the overwhelming sense of failure that comes with explaining why no one has called back. So I tell them where I applied, adding it to the list of places I won't work, and we never talk about that company again. It's healthy. But that's not to say there isn't advice. Advice abounds.

Being unemployed while living at home is a breeding ground for suggestions.

Looking for a job in general is one of those instances in life where people feel inclined to put in their two cents. Like when men gather around a fire telling each other the best way to start it. And people who think they know you best are there to constantly remind you of talents you seem to be forgetting. The main reason for this lapse is most likely that these are talents you've never once possessed. But you can't tell them that. So you smile and say thank you, and tell them that you'll look for a job designing floral arrangements tomorrow.

Obviously, my parents are the co-founders of this club. Despite the fact that I usually can't think of a single response to about 85% of the things they say, they've continued to offer suggestions in hopes that something will peak my interest. The other night while watching a show about Ireland, my father asked in all seriousness if I'd ever consider getting involved with Riverdance. I looked at him until I was sure he wasn't kidding and then proceeded to look up at the ceiling and inhale slowly. This has become a daily practice. I've never been more aware of ceilings than during this stretch at home.

When the comments don't cease, I scan the room looking for anyone who might have seen or heard the suggestion. It's narcissistic to think that it's possible, but most days I feel like my life is being recorded for the purposes of a hidden camera show. So after nearly everything my parents say, I search the room waiting for the cameramen and producers to run out. It has yet to happen.

I brace myself everyday at noon for such suggestions. My dad came rushing into the house the other day with an exaggerated smile and tossed me a catalog. "Here, Jess. I think I'm going to get these for you."

I looked at what appeared to be golf shoes with large metal spikes on the soles. I stared at the picture and waited for an explanation. In most instances, he would rather save than spend, but give him a catalog and he's ready to shop. The man will hold on to the same pair of sneakers for three years, but somehow a $600 toaster seems like a good idea. It's lucky Deb and Steve don't travel much because I could see him justifying all of his Sky-Mall purchases with duty-free arguments. The most useless things gain profound importance for him when put onto thin glossy pages. He would, without a doubt, go out of his way to mention the 'Advanced Large Capacity Feline Drinking Fountain' despite the fact that we don't even have a cat.

Pointing at the shoes on the page he said, "This way, you can kill two birds with one stone. Have fun walking and aerate the lawn!"

Listening to my father talk is similar to playing Three Card Monte without knowing which card I'm supposed to follow. It's just a random shuffle leaving me unsure as to what I should identify. I didn't know how lawn aeration related to anything so I simply agreed to think about the spike shoes and joined him at the island to listen to him eat a sandwich and hear about his day. He was talking about hauling cabbage leaves to a cow farm or something of the like and interrupted himself saying, "I know! Why not try a chicken place!" It took a few seconds to realize he was talking to me.

"Sorry?"

"Yeah, why not apply to a chicken place? I don't know, just a thought."

For all the money in the world, I could not, at that moment, conjure up the emotional strength to ask him what the hell he was talking about. What is a chicken place? Seriously, what does that even mean? Inhaling slowly, feeling my lungs fill to a painful capacity, I tilted my head up and stared at the kitchen ceiling. It's my favorite ceiling in the house. I didn't say anything, but there's a strong possibility my father thinks my future awaits me at a Chik-Fil-A.

Later that night my mother prepared tacos for dinner. The fact that I comment on the way they eat their food—namely that it seems to end up all over them—has created a semi-hostile environment around meal times. My mom gets upset that I won't just sit still and enjoy dinner, but instead play base coach, pointing to my face, my chest, my face, letting them know where they have food. I get upset because I can't have a serious conversation with someone when they have taco shell on their cheek. As she set up a toppings bar, I agreed to set up a real bar, making margaritas. Tacos are messy. The only way I was going to get through this meal in a civil, no-comment fashion was with alcohol.

As usual, my unemployment was the topic of casual dinner conversation. The tequila made me not mind so much. Perhaps it was because of the tequila that I actually asked them both what they thought I should do. Applying to so many jobs and coming up empty handed, I was open to their recommendations. There was a bit of a pause and then my father looked up from his plate and began to speak in a serious tone. Could it be? Was he actually going to offer a helpful suggestion?

"Jess," he said, speaking slowly, "I really think that if you work hard and set the goal, you can go to Mars by the time you're thirty." And then he returned to his taco.

Tolstoy writes of an "arrest of life." This was mine. If I were the star of *The Wonder Years* and not Fred Savage, this would be the point that my older me voice over would have nothing to say. The suggestion of Mars was completely unreasonable but that wasn't the problem. The problem was that he was serious. I have a bachelor's in film, I'm living at home with my parents and I haven't taken an advanced math course since high school. Why not go to Mars? That's exactly the type of advice I've been seeking. Why didn't any of my advisors pick up on this at school?

I sat at the table dumbfounded, watching my father sloppily eat his taco, food all over his face. *You have food ON YOUR FACE! Don't you feel it?! Sour cream, pieces of shredded lettuce hanging from your face! You're making me sick!* I had to look away. My eyes followed mom as she moved to the blender for more margarita. Watching her pour the last of it into my glass I realized she never commented on the Mars plan. Not even a slight roll of the eyes to dismiss it. Was it possible she agreed? It occurred to me that this entire night

had to be for the show. I looked behind me and to the surrounding rooms and waited to be swarmed by lights and
boom mics. Waiting on the edge of my chair I finally said,
"Unless I'm shot into space, I don't see how you can do any
better than this!"

This she heard, and my mother asked with concern
who I was talking to. Getting up to make another blender of
margaritas, I answered in finger quotes, "Nobody."

NAPS AND NIHILISM

I was lying on the sofa doing nothing the other day when Vanessa came in and sat on me. Not saying anything for a few minutes, she finally got up to leave. When she came back into the living room a little later I had the strongest sense of déjà vu.

"I just had déjà vu!" I said.

"No kidding," she replied. "You do this everyday."

Trying to figure out the direction in which I should point my life has not been easy. There are so many disclaimers, or footnotes, or variables to everything in life that as soon as I establish something for myself, another part of me chimes in with a doubting tone. It's created an awkward duality where I'm not really sure what to believe. So in an effort to help myself, I'm attempting to de-clutter my head, only keeping the things I really need. In the same way that every item of clothing in a closet must be questioned before clearing it out, all my old beliefs about what holds value are being put to the test. When was the last time I wore these jeans? What do I really know for sure? That sort of thing. Note to reader: This incessant internal questioning and/or treating your head like a closet will drive you insane.

I've slipped into a dark period of introspection

where everything I establish for myself is called into question. Even showers have fallen under the "What's the point?" scrutiny. I don't have anywhere to be during the day so why would I take part in that energy wasting cycle? Dry, clothed, naked, wet, dry, clothed. It seems like too many steps to end up right back where I started. After I decide not to shower, my passions, my goals, and my beliefs are all brought in for questioning. They sit in a cramped room with a bright lamp and a two-way mirror where I interrogate them for hours. I'm not even sure what I'm looking for by doing this. Maybe I'm hoping to catch my old ideas in a lie because I'm not thrilled about where they've gotten me. I really don't know. But in the meantime it's a game of Good Cop/Bad Cop as I attempt to verify what I really value and what I really know. The result is mental paralysis and exhaustion.

It would be so nice to have something in my head that could withstand my questioning nature. I'd like to be able to make an assertion about anything that is as clear and true as those made in *Richard Scarry's Best Word Book Ever*. I've been thinking a lot about that book lately. As far as word books go, it really was the best ever. I love the idea of everything having a name, a place, and a function without needing further written explanation. Cup. Saucer. Plate. Bowl. Fork. Knife. Spoon. Glass. What a wonderfully simple and clear way of looking at the contents of the world. Free from doubt, unchained to the contrary, just things as they are.

I used to request *Best Word Book Ever* as a bedtime story almost exclusively when I was young despite the fact that it didn't exactly read well as a linear tale. I think at one point the book moved from a detailed account of what the Pig Family ate at their holiday meal, to a comprehensive list of boats and ships. I don't remember noticing the randomness in that at all. Not caring about the absence of segue is such a great thing about being a kid. Besides, bedtime stories were never really about plot, they were about bedtime. And listening to a role call of objects was a strange sort of lullaby. I found comfort in the cadence of everyday things. I miss that. I miss being able to look at the things that surround me with full confidence in their truth.

It's draining to look at what you once knew to try to find out what you know, but even more tiring is listening to yourself. So as I slip deeper into my woe-is-me existential crisis, I nap. I've been napping a lot. I figure that if I keep turning over I can stay asleep for 22 hours. Well, maybe the math is a little fuzzy, but still. I'd like to think my situation is not unique and that other young adults fresh out of college are also tired all the time, but I fear it might just be me. I remember hearing about mono for the first time and its symptoms of a general lack of energy and I thought to myself, "Oh my God, I have mono. I've had mono since I was like eight."

In the interest of full disclosure, I should mention that I do love naps. Sartre said, "Three o'clock is always too late or too early for anything you want to do," and I have to agree. One should never take for granted the beauty and simple perfection behind the uninterrupted nap. When meeting people who are completely anti-nap, I'm inclined to ask them what their problem is. It's like people who say they never liked *Seinfeld*. They can be the salt of the earth, but when I hear that I know I'll never be giving them the "Be Fri" half of my Best Friends necklace.

College is wonderful in that it creates an accepting and supportive environment for mid-day, early evening, and post 8:00 AM class siestas. It'd be hard to find such a welcoming atmosphere anywhere else on the planet. Take for instance, the power nap. Academia has elevated the nap to such a level of importance as to suggest ideas of power. If you will, picture yourself or someone you know napping. That something consisting of lying down with a blanket should evoke images of power is an idea born and sustained in college. The greatness surrounding it all is that you're free to nap when you deem it necessary. It's something more schools should consider putting in brochures. People slept whenever they wanted to in college, and no one said anything. Taking naps at home, however, is like sitting next to a vegan at a barbecue. Any enjoyment is trumped by the looks of judgment.

My mother came home yesterday to find me still lying on the sofa.

"Um, Jess, have we moved today?"

"Yes! I didn't wake up here did I?" As she walked away I had to ask myself, did I?

I don't know why she's so upset to find me in the same position on the couch for eight hours a day. Yes, I'm bored, I'm depressed, and upset with what my life has become, but at least I'm not making it everyone else's problem. I send all the invites to my Pity Party to myself. And when I eventually grow disgusted with my own complaints, I fall asleep. I don't know why people waste thousands of dollars in therapy when all they need is a softer blanket and two new pillows. Problem solved. They'll feel better because they're well rested, and everyone around them will feel better because they can't hear them.

It's a gorgeous day outside so I grab an iced tea and head for the front porch, if only to avoid hearing my mother tell me that it's a gorgeous day outside. When you're depressed, people are always telling you that it's a gorgeous day outside, like that's going to miraculously change your mood. I feel bad for depressed people in San Diego. That must get really annoying, hearing that everyday. My mom follows me out and sits on the Adirondack chair next to me.

"Jess," she says, "I don't like this. You're sleeping all day, you never leave the house, I'm really concerned."

I nod in agreement. "Yeah, me too."

"I'm serious, Jessica."

"Yeah, me too." I say it with wider eyes this time to emphasize that I really mean it.

"So talk to me. How can I help?"

Her question sort of lingers. I'm watching cars drive by the house while trying to think of an answer. It occurs to me that even if I wanted her help I wouldn't know how to describe the problem. I guess if I had to give it a name I'd call it whining. That's probably why I've been trying to work out what I'm feeling on my own, because it seems so silly to ask someone to help you stop whining.

"Truthfully mom," I say, "I feel like I'm flailing around inside my head. I'm completely overwhelmed by my own lack of knowledge. I worked so hard throughout school but I can't find a job anywhere. I didn't see that coming. I grew up listening to you say that I could be whatever I wanted to be, only to just recently realize that I have no fucking clue what that is. I probably should have thought about that earlier, huh? Everyone keeps asking me where I'm going and the question gives me vertigo. Where am I going? Seriously. Where? I have one foot stuck in a puddle of the past, while the other is in a mound of crap that is my present. So I'm not exactly glowing with anticipation for the future. I'm so confused, I don't even recognize myself."

Only, I don't actually say this. I think about saying it. I think about mentioning something about how Kierkegaard said that "Anxiety is the dizziness of freedom" and that maybe I'm feeling like this because of too many options. But I realize how stupid it all sounds. I feel guilty about my complaints so I simply say, "I don't know, Mom. I guess I'm just tired."

She looks perplexed and asks, "How can you be tired? Didn't you just get up?"

This is a common fissure in our attempts to understand each other. It's rooted in my inability to share exactly what's on my mind and my mother's quite literal interpretation of the things that I do say. I have somewhat of an existential view towards life that she sees as overly pessimistic, so it's hard to open up when I know the conversation will end with her saying I'm being morbid. I like to consider myself a realist while she thinks of me more as a fatalist. But if I am fatalist, is it any wonder? My Uncle Jerry used to send us these nature videos called, "The Trials of Life," and we'd watch them in horror. While other kids my age were singing along with Disney movies we were watching the real lion king graphically devour a pack of unsuspecting gazelles. There's no catchy tune to accompany that visual.

A few minutes pass without a single car driving by the house and I notice the silence. I look at my mom, who is just sort of sitting there patiently, waiting for me to talk if I want. Front porches are nice in that respect. If you're sitting on a porch, chances are you don't have anywhere to be and porch conversation is never in a big hurry either. I sink lower into my Adirondack chair and look at the ice cream stain on my shorts. How long has that been there?

"You know," I say, breaking the quiet, "the other day when we were at the mall I saw a balloon hitting the ceiling. I've seen it a hundred times before but something about that balloon floating in the expanse of that high ceiling made me so sad."

"Yeah," my mom says. "Especially when you think of how far that kid who was holding it had to fall."

She waited for me to appreciate her joke, which I did. My mother knows when to snap me out of introspective moods, and a dose of her humor usually helps. She's quite hilarious when she wants to be and solved many an argument when we were kids by employing said skill. Whenever my sisters and I fought she would sit us down, make us stare at each other and instruct, "No laughing!" Of course we lasted around three seconds and forgot what we were so upset about because staring contests are the height of hilarity. And if we were ever mad at her? Forget about it, we didn't have a chance. After two minutes of yelling about the lack of fairness in our lives she would put on an extreme look of concern, nod slowly, and proceed to lift her nose up like a pig snout, without so much as blinking. If anyone can continue an argument when the other party is forcing pig nose, you obviously have no sense of humor. This stupid maneuver added immediate levity and put everything in perspective. I truly think pig nose should be used as a common form of conflict resolution. (Note: Pig nose does not work in instances of carjacking, street fights, or armed robbery. These people tend to be serious and find nothing amusing about exaggerated nostrils.)

My mom mentions that the balloon reference seems straight out of an art house film. Speaking with a German accent she goes on to suggest that my life be made into a movie called, *The Recluse*, and proceeds to dictate the opening lines:

"Zee girl vakes up from her ninth nap of zee day. She searches for a pair of shorts—oh vait—the one's she has on vill do. She eats her cereal and contemplates zee meaning of it all. She does not know. She decides to take a nap and sink about it in tventy minutes. She is zee Prophet of Doom. And she likes it."

"Very funny, mom. You're incredibly sharp."

"And you smell. Take a shower and let's go out to eat."

"When?"

"Six o'clock. That gives you an hour to put pants on. Get in that shower, Prophet."

Out to dinner my mother asks if I'd recommend any of the books I've been reading lately. She's made it quite clear that she thinks I've become too involved with the books I read, so I'm curious as to why she brings it up. For an entire week after I finished reading a biography on Stephen Hawkins, she interrupted me every time I started to speak by asking, "Is this about Black Holes again?" But the public library has been my saving grace. I don't even want to think about the levels of boredom to which I might have stooped had it not been for the beauty of free books.

"Um, well you probably wouldn't like anything I've

been reading lately."

"I like almost anything, try me."

"Well actually I was digging through some of my old philosophy texts and I've stared reading Nietzsche again."

"Oh, good for the beach."

"Exactly."

"Jess, I don't think you should read Nietzsche right now. You're not quite Mary Sunshine at the moment and reading endlessly about nihilism isn't really what you need, is it?"

"I don't know. Maybe all my doubts and insecurities about things will lead me to a greater understanding. Nietzsche wrote that a form of nihilism was experienced before people could truly know how much value their values and ideals really held."

My mom nods quickly and says, "Well, what did Nietzsche say about the lobster roll? Because that sounds good."

Remember those Life cereal commercials when the businessman or woman ate the cereal for breakfast and then shrunk down to become a little kid, still in their grown-up clothes? I feel like this is how all parents view their children. So I imagine when you're 35-years-old, speaking to your parents, they'll look at you with puzzled expressions thinking, "Why are you wearing those clothes? They're obviously too big for you." Because is it me, or do all parents maintain confused looks when listening to their kids? I think it stems from the fact that what we expect from each other is so categorically different in every sense that it puts an unspoken strain on communication. We expect our parents to be reliable, present both emotionally and financially, understanding, forgiving, all-knowing, and witty at appropriate times. But all of these things are footnoted with the idea that they'll do them and never make it known. Just do it, don't tell me about it. Parents on the other hand, expect us to be happy.

And really, which is the harder of the two? The child's expectations may seem unreasonable but at least we're specific. The parent's expectation is so incredibly vague that when we're not happy, they take it as a personal affront.

So between what we need from each other and how we relate to each other, it's a wonder we communicate effectively at all. And let's be honest, when communication is a success, it's usually about food. My family uses food the way that other families use duct tape. It's the solution to nearly every problem. When I say, "I think I'm a failure and I'm experiencing feelings of nothingness" my parents see me in an oversized business suit with gigantic shoulder pads. When I say, "I'm hungry" we've opened up the floodgates of communication.

—Do you want a snack or a meal?

—Should I make sauce?

—Do you feel like Chinese? Oh, China Buffet?

Food—specifically China Buffet—could be an answer to nine out of ten questions asked to my parents, regardless of the topic. They have a brilliant spin-doctor sense of dialogue in this respect and can turn almost any query into an impassioned speech about the wonders of all-you-can-eat crab legs. I'd like to contact the makers of Magic 8 Ball to see if they could make "China Buffet" one of the answers. "It is decidedly so." "Doubtful." "China Buffet." I can't think of a more appropriate gift for the two of them.

Looking around the restaurant I wonder if anyone else is confronted by feelings of nothingness; stripping away all that they once knew to find out what they now know. The waitress interrupts my narration of this scene of *The Recluse* and my mother orders.

"I'll have the lobster roll. Jess, did you want to order, or is there really no point since you'll be hungry again in the morning?"

Waving off the fact that she read my mind, I order the same.

"I DON'T KNOW, MARGOT!"

I've never been good with small talk. Talking in general tends not to be my strong point. The problem lies in my complete inability to reprimand my inner child. I could be having a semi-normal conversation with someone, and then think of something totally unrelated to the topic that for some reason strikes me as very funny. So I'll think only of that until I either (a) Burst out laughing awkwardly or (b) Say it aloud and confuse the other party, leaving them no choice but to walk away. Things like sleeping bags tend to pop into my mind at random times, which, on the whole, are not very funny. But when you shouldn't be thinking about sleeping bags, and should be actively listening to someone, sleeping bags can really get the giggles going. Particularly if you envision the person you're talking to standing up in a sleeping bag. Clearly, I'm eight years old.

In discussion groups in college, I was amazed by how much my fellow peers could talk. They could go on and on for entire classes. At first I thought they were incredibly brilliant, but when I actually started listening I realized they weren't saying much at all. These pontificators were usually drama majors or high on something, and if they happened to be both, I would get up and walk out. Not to hate on drama majors; I just have trouble listening to people speak louder than necessary with perfect diction. It annoys me. Drama majors in my classes were very good at flawlessly enunciating their long responses, which somehow always ended up being about James Lipton. Maybe that was just my experience.

Students who showed up high were only slightly less annoying because they offered a bit of comic relief, but even that started to wane after 90 minutes. I remember once in a Philosophy of Religion class the professor started to discuss awe, and what would inspire awe. A student raised his hand and said, "If a pod of whales swam into the room right now I would be like, whoa." And he went on to explain why. Yeah, we get it. It would be weird to see whales in the classroom.

Nietzsche said that "When speaking of what is great, one must either be silent or speak with greatness." I always thought this was spot on and found myself, more often than not, opting to stay silent because it's very hard to think on my feet about how I might weave sleeping bags into greatness. However, since leaving college I've been confronted daily by small talk with people I haven't seen in years and I can't really stay silent in those situations. My first instinct is always to run away, but it is written somewhere in social graces that you can't run away from people when they're talking to you. So I stand there, attempting not to picture them as little zippered up pigs-in-a-blanket, hoping the conversations will end quickly.

Graduates, pregnant women, and people with large visible casts all share something in common: Being approached by people to whom they'd otherwise not like to speak. And whether they mean well or not, these people will suffocate the graduate/pregnant/injured with questions. What happened to your leg? Is it a boy or a girl? So what are you doing now?

And while the woman swollen with child or the

man rolling in traction may outwardly appear to be in more discomfort, it is in fact the graduate who will suffer the most once the initial question is launched into the universe.

Boy/girl, hiking accident/hit by a bus—pick one. People really don't care. But the recent college graduate has no such luxury. "I'm not quite sure" is nowhere near an acceptable reply. "Taking some time off" is as good as answering in some sort of clicking language. Relatives, old acquaintances, and complete strangers will all look at you the same way. With their heads tilted and their eyes narrowed, they'll examine you like they're looking at a Pollack and waiting for the value and meaning to jump out at them but then—nope, nothing. Just a big mess. Then they'll force a smile the way people do at dinner parties when they've noticed undercooked chicken but don't want to embarrass the host. It's an equal parts combination of incomprehension and poorly-masked disgust.

The first twenty times this happened I was confused. I started to replay the conversations in my head making sure I didn't accidentally say something heinous.

"Well, I majored in film so I'll be drowning kittens for the summer." No, I definitely did not say that.

The sudden interest other people had in my life, followed by their tangible disappointment confounded me up until the twenty-first time I was asked, "So what are you doing now?" At this time I was introduced to a rage that no one had told me about. The post-graduate, "No, what are YOU doing now?" rage for which the Career Center at Syracuse offered no flyer. I reached a boiling point of bafflement as to why people seemed to care so much. I just couldn't wrap my head around the idea that these people were so upset when I didn't have a solid answer for them. Isn't it common knowledge that catch-up chit chat is just something you do to be polite? Say hello, how are you, and move on. It's not the damn Inquisition! I began to take small-talk questions personally and moved into the most unassuming of conversations with my defenses up. And I've never been one for small talk anyway, so to have to worry about the questions and ultimate dissatisfaction of people I bump into at the bank or the post office has made me more nervous than usual.

I was at a friend's graduation party a few weeks ago where I was surrounded by all the typical questions. It blows my mind when strangers ask what I'm doing, with their condescending remarks and trite comments about the economy, giving me well-wishing pats on the back. Thanks. Now please go away. It got so bad that by the end of the party I just began to be brutally honest.

"Well, I get up around noon to watch TV and if I take a shower, I consider the day a success. Otherwise, I do nothing until I fall asleep and then I do it all over again the next day. I'll probably keep that schedule going through the summer, or until my parents kick me out of their house. Whatever comes first."

Each person's reply started with an elongated pause, like they were waiting for the joke, but when they finally realized there was no punch line, they smiled and quickly walked away. Questioning a practicing loser on her career goals makes people very uncomfortable, and rightfully so. I just met you. How could you possibly care what I'm doing? Ask me where I got this plate of chips and salsa. Ask me where the bathroom is. But don't bring up a line of questioning that only reaffirms what I'm not doing. I get enough of that at home.

I've been thinking about the scene in *National Lampoon's Christmas Vacation* where the Griswolds' snobby neighbors come home to find their window broken. Clark Griswold accidentally shoots a roof gutter full of ice through his neighbor's bedroom window, destroying a stereo, and the ice eventually melts on the floor. While cleaning up the mess, Julia Louis Dreyfus' character, Margot, asks, "And why is the carpet all wet, Todd?" To which Todd replies, "I don't know, Margot!"

I channel my rage through this single line of dialogue because it seems to fit so perfectly with my situation. My life after graduation has played out much like finding a destroyed stereo on a wet carpet and attempting to make sense of it. When people ask what I intend to do with the mess before I've had a chance to figure out what's happened, it causes unnecessary stress. When questions of life direction are unleashed, I mentally scream, "I don't know, Margot!" and allow it to echo through the caverns of my mind.

"So what will you do with your life?"

"I don't know, Margot!"

"What's next for you, college grad?"

"I don't know, Margot!"

With the mantra resounding in my head, I smile and do the bizarre, *friendly laugh at nothing* chuckle. You know the one. It follows finishing a huge meal at a restaurant when the server comes over to ask if you'd like dessert and instead of just saying no, you laugh strangely.

"Would you care for some dessert?"

"Ohhhh no. Hahaha. We really couldn't. Hahaha. But thank you."

An offer for dessert is not funny, but for some reason the suggestion of confection after a large meal demands that we employ that awkward laugh. The only way it would be funny—and I've thought about this—is if people had just finished eating tiramisu, brownies, and a big slice of red velvet cake at a pastry shop and upon handing them their check the waitress asks if they'd like to see a dessert menu. And even that is only mildly amusing because you know the waitress probably uses that line all the time. Perhaps I've actually thought about this too much.

Anyway, that awkward laugh is the subtle hint that the other party should move along, and it seems to work. Used in combination with screaming "I don't know Margot!" internally, the socially unpleasant, *too full for dessert* laugh, has been an effective way of getting those people and their questions away from me. I'm free to apply to jobs online at my leisure without the pressure of needing an answer for the inquiring minds of our small town.

Growing up in a small town is defined by various certainties that are simultaneously positive and negative. Example: People know you. That's positive. And also, people know you. That's negative. So when I'm walking through the grocery store and hear, "Jessica!" I pretty much know it's me. In a city, you're preconditioned to ignore the sound of your own name in public areas if only to avoid the awkward, "Oh, not me? Right, because we don't know each other." I choose to venture out to the grocery store or Wal-Mart as little as possible because to do so is to face a town of old teachers and the parents of old friends who want to know what I'm doing and it's hard to tell people who once had high hopes for you that you're now living in perpetual pajama bottoms.

You know you've reached a new low when you're darting across aisles to avoid saying hi to someone you actually like.

But I'm feeling confident with my new technique. It's amazing how quickly people will end a conversation that is teeming with uncomfortable laughter. I'm feeling so confident, in fact, that I've decided to join Vanessa and my mother at one of the local hotspots. Any restaurant that has more than three "platters" on the menu is a hotspot in Brockport. I think this place has six. Someone once told me that if you sat at a café along the Champs d'Elysees long enough, you'd see everyone in Paris pass by. I don't know how much truth there is to that, but if you sat at a booth in this place for ten minutes, you'd see half the people in my town. There's something to be said for that. I'm just not sure what it is.

The three of us are sitting in the restaurant, enjoying rolls and butter and waiting for our salads to be brought out on the clear plastic plates that look like lettuce. Our table faces the entrance and when the chain of bells on the door jingles, I look up to see a friend of mine from high school and her mother walk in. Great. I hadn't kept in touch since we went off to college, but she had remained on my Buddy List through the years so I still knew everything I needed to know about her through away messages. Not just her, everyone. Every twenty minutes at school, taking a break from writing papers to check the away messages of people I once knew.

Let's see what Johnny's up to.

"Eating Lunch."

Oh, good to know Johnny still likes lunch.

And later, after he's been idle for 6h38m. Well, I guess there's a chance that message could have changed.

"Eating Lunch."

Nope, guess not.

And it's not a stalker thing. It was just a way to make sure that what I was doing was on par with what everyone else was doing. If so-and-so said they were napping at noon, I didn't feel so bad about doing the same thing. And if what's her face was watching *Maury*, I suddenly had an elevated sense of self and my morning game show addiction. I mean, seriously, *Maury*? How can you watch that crap?

I wonder if there is a chance my old friend won't see me in this tiny restaurant.

Me: I should probably go say hello, right?

Mom: Of course.

Walking over I tell myself not to mention the breakup with her boyfriend that I had read all about. That was really beautiful though, when you guys got back together. I loved that song you quoted in your profile. Something like, "But you can still hit it in the morning." That was really special.

Me: Hey! Long time!

Girl: Yeah, I know! (Awkward hug)

Girl's Mom: So how are you?

Me: Really well, thanks. How—

Girl's Mom: I read in the paper you finished school. A year early, huh?

Me: Um, yeah. Well I had the credits so I figured…

Girl's Mom: So you must have had a job lined up then, huh?

Me: Haha. (*Dessert? Thank you, no.*)

Girl's Mom: You're not living here now are you?

Me: Here? No. We just came here for food.

Girl's Mom: Well I meant Brockport, silly.

Me: Haha. (*I'm much too full to hear about the cake specials.*)

Girl and her mother: Blank Stares.

Me: Um, well, right now I'm at home. It's been a real treat (*Just the check. HAHA*)

Girl's Mom: But what exactly are you doing now? (*Why is the carpet all wet Todd?*)

Me: Well, I've been reading a lot. (*I DON'T KNOW, MARGOT!*)

Girl's Mom: Reading?

Me: Well, I'm going to go finish dinner. Nice to see you both.

I return to the table bright red and sweating.

"What's wrong with you?" Nessa asks.

Rubbing my forehead I lean in to whisper, "She wouldn't let up. She just kept asking and asking. Why the fuck does she care what I'm doing?"

"Oh, stop," my mom says, waving her hand as if swatting a fly. "She's just being friendly."

"Mom, I'm sweating. Look at me! When was the last time friendly banter gave you pit stains? I feel sick. Can we go?"

Nessa chimes in with an instigating smile, "I was kind of looking forward to that Reuben Platter. We should probably stick around."

We stay and I silently pray she doesn't come over to our table.

Our food arrives and the rest of the meal continues without incident. However, just as we shift in our seats getting ready to leave, I feel a hand on my arm. Shit.

"Hi Deb. So you've got the college grad at home, huh?" The woman squeezes my forearm when she says this and I can feel myself start to sweat again.

"Yeah," my mom says, "we're pretty lucky."

Yeah! Thanks Mom!

And then this girl's mother bends down literally inches from my face, still holding my arm and says, "But really, Jessica. What is it that you're doing right now?"

I wait for another helpful comment from my mother. And wait. And wait.

You know that moment when you go to sit down on a chair and realize it's not there? How that fall to the ground plays out slowly as you think, I should have hit chair by now? That three-second sit-down is a twenty-five second slow-motion disaster.

This moment, waiting for an answer to this woman's question was four days. Suns rose, suns set. Pancake platters were served, hamburger platters were cleared away. Nothing. Until finally the sound of my sister's voice snaps me back to real time.

"Yeah, Jess. What *do* you do all day?"

She says this with a smile that both mocks me and revels in my discomfort. I shoot her back a smile that says I hate you as I turn to the woman. Smiling wider now, I answer.

"Well, um, truthfully… I didn't want to talk about it because it's still in the early stages, but, uh, I'm starting a business." I grab a mint off the check tray and unwrap it, keeping my eyes locked with the woman.

"Really?" she asks.

"Yup. That's right." I pop the mint into my mouth while nodding. "Well, like I said, it's early. But the basic idea behind it, and um, I think there's certainly a market for it both domestically, as well as abroad, is traditional dance."

"Excuse me?" She loosens her grip on my arm and pulls her head back a bit.

"Yeah, well what we'll be doing is teaching traditional equine dance. That is, traditional classics—the Tango, the Cha-Cha, the Meringue—to horses. It's really an untapped market, pardon the pun. But the true challenge lies in actually getting the horses on their hind legs for the duration of the class. That's something we're working on. But truly, I'm very proud of it."

"What?"

"It's called, Hip Hip Horsay! We'll be advertising in the town paper so look for it. You read that one, right?"

And if life could be scripted I would have cued the waitress to come over at this moment and ask us if we wanted pie. And my mother, my sister and I would have roared with laughter at the suggestion.

Nonono, no pie. HA! We couldn't possibly! HA-HAHA.

But we had already paid so we just got up and left.

I'M NOT WELL

I think something is wrong with me. I was watching *The Price Is Right* yesterday and broke down crying when a contestant won $10,000 on Plinko. Clearly, this is a new low. But I think the lack of emotional equilibrium displayed in this outburst is simply the visible effect of more pressing physical problems. Lately I've been having intense chest pains and shortness of breath and I've stated almost daily that I'm having a heart attack.

The first time I mentioned this over breakfast everyone laughed in unison. This is the support system I'm working with. Granted, my family knows better than to indulge me. They know my history of hypochondria and understand that to agree with me even slightly is to set me into a panic.

Once after watching a documentary about Elephantiasis, I stared at my ankles every morning for a week with a real fear that they could expand at a moment's notice. And another time after driving with Vanessa for about sixteen hours straight on a road trip, my neurosis combined with lack of sleep to convince me that the sundae I was eating might have AIDS. I know it was ludicrous, but I hadn't slept in over a day. When I started to flip out Vanessa said, "Fine. Tomorrow we'll go to Planned Parenthood and when they ask you why you want an HIV test, just tell them it's very likely you contracted AIDS from a hot fudge sundae."

That was enough to snap me back to reality. Although since then, the sundae story is almost always thrown back in my face when I start to complain about any health problem—like heart disease, as is currently the case.

This was the scene from breakfast this morning:

Me: I'm having a heart attack.

Mom: No you're not.

Me: Seriously, I am.

Ness: When was the last time you had ice cream?

Me: Stop!

Ness: Maybe it's heartburn from all that hot sauce you put on everything.

Mom: Yes, that's it exactly. You probably have acid reflux. Case closed. Now stop rubbing your left arm.

It was a great comfort growing up in the presence of such a brilliant medical mind. My mother would have you believe that she is a doctor, despite the fact that all of her information comes from the pages of *Good Housekeeping* or *Prevention* magazine. I'm convinced my hypochondria stems from her random analyses, spewed out with no medicinal knowledge whatsoever. If I ever complained of feeling ill, a leap frog of diagnosis ensued until the worst possible cause was a distinct possibility. Her line of questioning always sounded something like, "You have a headache? OK. You might be dehydrated. Actually, are you having trouble seeing? Is it a very bad headache? You might have an aneurism." Or, "Why are your feet so cold? I think you might have poor circulation. Either that or, do you feel thirsty all the time? You might have diabetes."

It got to the point that any time I reached for a Kool-Aid I wondered if it was my diabetes making me do it. And I don't have diabetes.

My mother offered perhaps her most extreme medical opinion over the phone and a few thousand miles away, when I called her one night from London. I was very nervous and in quite a great deal of pain due to the fact that I hadn't—how to put this delicately? — pooped in eight days. I know what you're thinking, that it's not possible. Well, it happened and it was horrible. The events that followed were not much better.

After telling my mom about my condition, she exclaimed, "Oh Jesus, Jessica!" You need to get to the hospital immediately! You have a bowel obstruction! You could die!"

Now, a person who hasn't gone to the bathroom for this long knows that there's something wrong. Telling them that their death is imminent does very little to help the situation, despite what certain catch phrases about being scared might have you believe. I rushed to the hospital thinking I had minutes left to live. Going to a hospital in a foreign country is intimidating no matter what, however, given the intimate level of embarrassment this visit involved, I was relieved in that I was in England and spoke English fluently. I can't even begin to imagine how that conversation would have played out in broken French.

While I waited in the lobby, my mother kept calling my cell phone for updates.

"What's going on?!" she demanded. The volume of her voice bellowed out of my phone like a car alarm and everyone in the waiting area looked over at me.

I tried to balance out the noise by whispering. "I'm waiting to see a doctor."

She shouted again, "Waiting?! Tell them it's an emergency!"

I pressed the phone harder against my head to muffle her voice and softly said, "Mom, this is the emergency room. They know."

Maintaining the urgency in her voice she said, "But Jess, you could…"

I was praying she wouldn't say explode.

"You could be very sick!"

Still whispering, I said, "Mom, I'm sitting two seats away from a man who's bleeding from his stomach. They'll get to me."

Unable to make my mother lower her voice, it occurred to me that if she was at the ER in London this entire conversation would have played out much like the scene in *Terms of Endearment*. My mom doing her own version of Shirley MacLaine, as she screamed around the nurse's station, "Get my daughter to poop! Get my daughter to poop!"

There were signs everywhere in the ER that read, "No mobiles" and the receptionist told me that if I didn't get off the phone they would take it. I told my mom to stop calling me and hung up.

When I finally met with a nurse for a pre-exam interview she asked me to explain the problem. I was really kicking myself for not taking more biology classes so I could have made it sound more sophisticated.

"Well," I said, "I have a bowel obstruction."

Widening her eyes a bit she asked, "And why do you think that?"

And it occurred to me, why *do* I think that? I knew shoving all those matchbox cars up my ass was a bad idea. Bowel obstruction! I'm an idiot for listening to my mom.

We discussed the problem and she asked me a series of questions to assess how I got to this point.

"Have you been eating fruit and veg?" she asked.

"Um, not so much," I replied.

"How much is that?"

"None."

"You're 20 years old, you should know to eat fruit and veg."

"I will never make that mistake again."

"How much do you drink a day?" she asked.

"Beer?"

"Water."

"Oh. I'm not quite sure."

"How many pints of beer?"

(Would extending my arms out to my sides and saying "This Many" be appropriate?) "Three." I lied.

I'll spare you the rest of the story but it involved the complete surrender of any pride I will ever have and some tubing. When I was walking out of the ER a nurse at the desk said, "Excuse me, are you Jessica?" This was great. Everyone there knew about the American girl who couldn't poop. Literally drained of everything, including my dignity, I answered in the affirmative with a defeated nod.

"Your mum rang twelve times."

It was during this experience—the worst in my life—that I came to a realization. First, a diet consisting exclusively of Muesli and Guinness will wreak havoc on your digestive system. But more importantly, I learned to never believe my mother's medical opinion.

So for the simple fact that she has been telling me that I'm not having heart attacks, I am all the more convinced that I am. Although, maybe it's something else entirely. I'm not blind to the fact that I might be searching for an illness at this particular time in my life to use as an excuse for my unemployment. It would be nice to have something to tell people besides, "I don't do anything."

"Where do you work?"

"Nowhere, I'm on dialysis."

Grabbing my chest as I try to make my case again, my mother finally suggests I see a doctor.

I never got around to changing my doctor when I went off to school so I scheduled an appointment at my pediatrician's office. Sitting on the short paper-lined table browsing through a year-old issue of *Highlights*, it strikes me that it might be a bit odd to complain of heart attacks in a room with Cookie Monster chairs. But I've been in situations more awkward than this. I've come to accept that anytime I step into a doctor's office I'm sure to make an ass of myself.

Once during a dermatologist visit I was given what I thought was a paper gown and told to put it on. Looking at it for a moment trying to figure out how I would step into it, I finally took off my pants and went leg first into a hole. Struggling to figure out how the gown should be worn, the doctor knocked at the door and it suddenly occurred to me, "She's looking at my neck. Why the hell are my pants off?" I yelled at her not to come in as I tried to get my leg out of what was actually a paper crop top.

I dismiss that thought as my chest grows tight again. Something is seriously wrong. I'm trying to settle myself but it's hard to do inside this little room. Plus, I can't seem to escape the googly-eyed stare of the Cookie Monster chair directly across from me and it's starting to freak me out. *What are you looking at? Never seen a grown girl with heart trouble in a pediatrician's office before?*

The Nurse Practitioner walks in and we exchange pleasantries as she poorly disguises her complete disbelief that I am consulting with a children's doctor.

"Are you pregnant?" she asks.

"What? Um, no."

"OK, why are you here?"

"I'm having heart attacks," I say, immediately wishing I phrased it differently.

There is a long pause followed by what I think is a glance at the Cookie Monster chair, as if to say, "Oh boy, Cookie Monster, here we go." This is followed by me glancing at both her and the character chair with widened eyes and hands on my chest as if to say, "No, seriously, you guys."

She listens to my heart, asking me to take deep breaths as she quickly moves the stethoscope before I've had a chance to exhale. I hate when doctors and nurses do this. Are they just trying to mess with me? They say, "take a deep breath" and then move that thing around so fast I'm left looking like a jerk trying to keep up with it using staccato inhales. Every time it moves I wonder if I should breathe out a little or just try to keep inhaling. "Deep breath." (Move.) "Deep breath." (Move.) "Deep breath." (Move.) Where are the instructions to exhale? As I feel myself start to puff up like an air mattress, I think of the direction waiters give diners as they stand over their salads with a peppermill—"Tell me when!"

I describe the symptoms of what I've been experiencing: cold sweats, shortness of breath, intense pains in my chest, and brace myself for the bad news. She scribbles notes furiously in the manila folder of my life. Years of medical notes, which must have included: "Child enjoys Kool-Aid, believes there is a medical issue there." "Young lady is much too tall for the examining table. She should probably see a grown-up doctor now." And I could tell this latest addition to my file would read, "Believe patient was describing ailments to plastic chair. Nod slowly and make sure she leaves the building."

After examining her notes she pauses for a few moments. Finally she says, "Well, your heart sounds fine. Blood pressure is normal. You've just finished school, right?"

"Right," I say.

"So what are you doing now?" she asks.

Cue chest pain.

"What?" I ask.

"What are you doing now that school is over?"

You've got to be kidding me with this! Obviously I can't use the dialysis excuse with her. I'm getting warm and I feel that tightness. I wonder if I should ask her to check my vitals again now so she knows I'm not crazy. I just decide to answer. "Um, I'm living at home and looking for a job right now."

"Hmm, OK." She says, scribbling in my folder. What the hell is she writing in there? I'd like to get my hands on that thing. Probably twenty years worth of doodles and signatures repeated over and over.

Cue sweating, cue shortness of breath.

"Graduation," she finally says, "and taking this next step can be highly stressful. Plus, moving back home isn't necessarily the easiest thing in the world. It's very possible you're having panic attacks."

"What?"

"Or at the very least, you're allowing anxiety to make you physically uncomfortable. My best advice would be to relax."

"But all I do is relax. Truthfully, like, pajamas for days."

"Well, that's not healthy either," she says.

"Well neither is shoving boxes of cookies in your mouth without chewing."

"Excuse me?"

"Nothing."

"All I'm saying is that perhaps you feel you're on a tight schedule and not meeting that schedule is causing unnecessary stress. Just try to relax, and realize it's not a race. You'll feel better almost immediately, I'm sure of it."

After talking a while longer, I thank her for her time and head out through the lobby. It's a waiting room full of little kids with coughs and runny noses all playing with the toys the doctor's office has provided. Sick toys, I call them. I think these children would be better off playing with the rental shoes from a bowling alley. But their parents don't seem to mind as the kids pass each other the blocks covered in a little bit of their chickenpox or pinkeye. Normally, this would bother me, but I'm feeling a sudden sense of calm. Going to the pediatrician had really put things in perspective. I bet I'm the first pediatric patient to ever say that. But really, what was I getting so worked up about? It's not a race. She's right. I'm not in a race. I say it a few more times to myself as I leave.

Back at home, I decide to make cereal for lunch. Sitting at the island eating my third bowl of Trix, my father comes running into the house, smiling as wide as he can.

He stands across from me saying nothing, but keeping his wide smile steady. I've told myself that I'm no longer going to play along in these games where I'm left to question what is going on. It seems that if I say nothing, my dad will eventually break and let me in on whatever it is. This particular game is lasting longer than I expected but I keep on eating my brightly-colored meal and watch as his face starts to shake.

Talking through his teeth, he says, "Guess where I've been." He looks and sounds like the world's worst ventriloquist.

I stare at him flatly and continue to eat.

Breaking from the smile he says, "The dentist. And guess what? I have very healthy gums."

I nod slowly and pour a little more Trix to finish off the remaining pink milk in my bowl, but at this point it reminds me of gums, so I decide not to eat it. Pushing it away, I look back over to my dad and he immediately resumes his big grin.

I laugh with him for a second and then out of nowhere, I feel the tightness in my chest again. Crap. I'm trying to remember what had calmed me in the waiting room of the doctor's office. It's not a race. Right. I repeat that and breathe as my father continues to smile and dance a bit around the kitchen.

"Oh yeah. Healthy gums. Oh yeah. Healthy gums." He's making a song out of it.

It feels like I have a charley horse in my heart. You know the feeling when a vitamin or Tylenol gets stuck in your throat? The entire left side of my chest feels like a giant pill is lodged in there. I'm thinking about what the doctor said, knowing that it's probably just my head making my body feel uncomfortable. I'm remembering her advice so I can make this little attack go away. Relax, I tell myself. Relax. Just because you have no plans for your future, and you're currently listening to your dad sing about his gums, and earlier this afternoon you were talking to a chair—at your pediatrician's office—there's no reason to panic.

FLYING J, WE SALUTE YOU

Summer is approaching its end, and my family and I have made our way down to Florida to help Vanessa move into college. Oh, the days of packing for freshman year. All things Rubbermaid, the preached importance of shower caddies and flip-flops, everyone buying egg crates for their beds. Having done the college move many times before, we've worked the list of necessary freshman-year items down to a science. However, packing for Vanessa proved to be difficult thanks to a power grid failure throughout the entire state of New York the night before our road trip. My dad is always talking about the importance of having multiple flashlights in easily accessible areas around the house. It's a Public Service Announcement he repeats every time he needs a flashlight and can't find one. You'd think he'd listen more carefully to himself. So while squinting and bumping into furniture in the pitch-black dark, we slowly moved my little sister's life out of the house, into the cars, and down to the Sunshine State.

Our road trip to Florida was met with relatively few obstacles given our history. Once, on a trip down South for a wedding, my father ran over a tire that was in the middle of the road and nearly killed us all. And usually our trips include two-hour detours to find the cleanest public restrooms possible. It's not uncommon for my dad to ask locals to recommend, "a good restaurant with a nice bathroom." My parents are completely ridiculous when it comes to public restroom cleanliness. They would prefer to cause potential harm to their kidneys than use a gas station toilet. When we were young, my dad often stopped at hotels and told us to use the lobby bathroom. Turning to the three of us sitting in the back seat he'd instruct, "If anyone asks, your room number is 206." We didn't really have any of that on this trip, and we've managed to arrive on time for Nessa's freshman move-in.

Helping her unload her things and watching all the other students take their first steps of college life is like watching a favorite old movie I haven't seen in awhile. All these first-year kids seem to be very chill about everything, but I'm bursting with nostalgia. I feel like I'm back in summer camp. I mean, I never went to summer camp, but I imagine the first day of camp and the first day of college play out the same way: the grandiose welcoming committee, having your family help you unpack, meeting your bunkmates. Well, maybe everything except for the bunkmate part. That sounds a little dirty. But all of these things are overshadowed by the eagerness to start earning merit badges in flip-cup and beer pong. Vanessa is about to experience the best years of her life and she probably doesn't even know it yet. So as I'm helping her set up her room, I can't help but keep a goofy grin on my face. I'm looking at her the way people must look at someone who's about to walk in on their own surprise party. I'm just sort of giddy for her to figure out what's going on. She'll realize eventually, probably too late.

Our day is cut short by the pressing matters that need to be addressed at Vanessa's first Floor Meeting. No doubt the topics will include the Birthday Bulletin Board and ice-breaker name games. I think that schools schedule orientation meetings or floor meetings on move-in day as a way of kicking families out at a reasonable hour. Even clingy parents probably say goodbye after hearing the word "meeting," not wanting their child to miss any information about dorm fire safety. Little do they know, it's just 45-minutes of awkward getting-to-know-you activities, like trying to untangle a human pretzel. Ah, college.

It's a tradition in my family to draw out goodbyes as long as possible. It started as children at my cousin Jonathan's house. My sisters and I never really wanted to leave his house so we used to tell him to hide in our car so that his parents and our parents would have to look for him and therefore, we could stay a little longer. After enough time passed, my aunt would eventually say, "You guys should probably just get on the road," and we'd drive off. Then about five minutes later Jonny would pop up from the back seat and my parents would be forced to turn around and bring him back. We found we could tag an extra hour or so onto our visits this way.

I'm reminded of this now as we all stand in the lobby of Vanessa's dorm. Our arms are full with bags of sweatshirts and crap from the bookstore and we're drawing out our goodbyes as best we can. My mother is fighting back the tears that started somewhere in North Carolina on the trip down here, while my dad is handing Nessa all the money he can find in his pockets; "Oh, here's another three dollars. Oh, here's fifty cents, for laundry. Oh, a ten!" We all give her our final hugs, and then our for-real final hugs, and finally leave. We're dropping Sabrina off at the airport and then it's back on the road for me, Deb, and Steve.

We wave goodbye from the car, calling out, "Bye! Okay, bye! See ya! Bye!" twenty times or more as my dad refuses to press the gas pedal. Standing at the entrance of her building, Nessa shouts out to me, "Have fun at the Flying J, Jess!" With this, my dad pulls away and I'm left screaming out the window, "What's the Flying J?"

Leaving the campus, my mother in tears, my dad

asks for someone to mark down the mileage. My father thinks recording gas mileage and collecting toll receipts are the essence of travel. I look to Sabrina and demand that she tell me what the Flying J is. "I have no clue," she says. "But I'm glad I'm Flying *home*."

We drop her off at the airport and I settle in, realizing that in the history of drives, this one—with only my parents—will be the longest ever recorded. I truly don't know how Nessa did it for all those years both Brina and I were in school. The difficulty lies in the fact that my mother and father each live in their own mental environments and carry on as such in a third, actual environment. The result is three conflicting realities at constant battle with each other and I'm the only one who seems to pick up on the awkwardness of it all. It's a paradox of social anthropological ideas that I have yet to understand, much like a Wal-Mart Super Center. (I don't really see how it's natural to have both underwear and mozzarella sticks in the same cart, I just don't.) So attempting to have a coherent conversation with them is like talking to a person who has been on the Atkin's Diet for too long. Somehow the conversation is always steered toward what is going on in their exclusive world of protein and you end up discussing that though you're not sure why. *Well, we weren't talking about bacon, but thanks for bringing it up.*

Every ten minutes on the road we get a report of the odometer as it relates to the gas needle. With roughly 340 miles to the tank, it is all I can do to keep myself from jumping out of the vehicle—moving at 71mph at all times. [We bow our heads and give thanks to you, sweet and everloving cruise control.] Meanwhile, my mother is discussing breakfast and her plans for lunch. Normally, she'd pass the time reading tabloids, but I refuse to let her do so in my presence. As soon as a magazine is in her hands, she feels the need to talk about celebrities as if they are her friends.

"Oh, Jennifer, really, what were you thinking?"

she'll ask.

"Mom, who are you talking to?"

"Jess, did you know Kate was in Hawaii?"

"Who the hell is Kate?"

The two of them would also be inclined to sing and dance to music, but I prepared for that and supplied all of our listening material for the ride home prior to starting this trip. A parent dancing is in the same category as a parent eating breakfast in their pajamas. They obviously have every right to do so, but you'd just prefer they didn't. My parents both fell in love with that Mitsubishi commercial years ago, where the girl in the passenger seat does the robot. Since then, they've thought that every song that comes on the car radio is the song from that commercial and bust out with their best robots. In an effort to avoid 24 hours of watching that, I made a whole bunch of mixes.

"Why are all these songs so depressing?"

"So no one can dance."

"Oh come on, Jess. Do you have that robot song we like?"

To disguise my hell as a vacation, we stop at South of the Border. This place would have definitely appealed to me as a child; bright colors, animals wearing sombreros, rides and games, foods to which every internal organ waves a white flag, and cheap souvenirs. Growing up, it wasn't really a vacation until someone got a plastic ninja sword. But maybe I've grown jaded, because all I see is shit. This is the only place I've seen outside a dollar store where the crap that surrounds you is considered ambiance. My mom says that she came here as a girl and not much has changed. Not much has changed?! They haven't mopped since 1960. I bite my tongue and we walk around to get some lunch.

We end up stopping at a hotdog (restaurant?) place, and order three hotdogs and fries. The overabundance of filthy tables leaves us to either stand or sit next to an air conditioner leak. It's the first time I've eaten surrounded by traffic cones, and aside from the semi-hypnotic sound of the drip drip drip, the periodical splash of water to the brow creates an outdoor experience, indoors. Waving flies off with one hand (is it me, or are there always flies wherever hotdogs are served?) and shoving our food down with the other, we finish our meal in record time. Buying a t-shirt at the gift shop, I consider my experience complete and we head back to the car.

Ten minutes down the road, with the attraction growing ever more south, I look out the window and smile. I think to myself how nice it will be nice to get back home, and the thought surprises me.

"OK, quarter of a tank," my dad announces. "About 103 miles. Can that be right, Jess?! This is fantastic gas!"

"God, that hotdog was good," my mom says, as she skips through all the slow songs on a CD, looking to find something with a beat. "I love a good hot."

And there goes the grin.

I fall asleep for a few hours before waking up to calls from the front seat telling me to sit up and get ready.

"Sit up, Jess! Here it comes!"

"Jess, wake up! Get ready!

"Get ready for what?"

But before I receive an answer the two of them place their right hands to their foreheads and say in unison, "Flying J, we salute you!" and proceed to salute a large sign that reads, "Flying J."

Oh, God. This is it.

As we pull off the exit and into the large parking lot full of semi-trucks and RVs, I fight the urge to comment on the salute, hoping we'll just get some gas and keep driving. But Nessa had warned me in that mordant wave goodbye. This might be awhile.

"Jess, you didn't salute," my dad says with disappointment.

"Dad, I'm not sure I have a response for that."

"It's the Flying J!" he says emphatically.

"Yes, I gathered. Does it have some sort of military affiliation?"

My parents turn and look at me. Their gazes demand to know, *Who is this girl? Surely she doesn't belong to us.*

"The Flying J! You know!" my mom insists.

Now I was getting pissed.

"No, I don't!"

A spark flashes in my father's eyes and he jumps out of the car shouting, "Then come on!"

The area surrounding the Flying J is a Peterbilt playground. Asphalt as far as the eye can see, the arresting smell of diesel, and the fluorescent glow of a sign advertising a 24-hour diner. My dad grabs my hand and rushes into the gift shop. Actually, calling it a gift shop might be underplaying it. It's a shop that sells food, souvenirs, clothes, tools, reading material, listening material, and basically anything else that you could ever need or never need during a road trip. One such example of the latter includes a foot-long plastic match that serves as a lighter. I can't tell you how many times I've been on the road and thought, damn, wish I had a foot long lighter.

I walk around the store while he continues to bring things over for me to look at.

"Look, Jess! Work gloves! Nice, right?"

"Yeah. Dad, what time is it?"

"A little after midnight, I think. Get some hot chocolate! Go ahead and grab some snacks. Oh, look at those! Would you like one of those t-shirts?"

He points to a series of t-shirts hanging on a wall that have various tractor-trailer trucks on them.

"No, I'm OK. Thanks."

"Well, they have so much stuff here, look around."

I'm afraid this stop officially confirms my suspicions that my parents are insane. I meet my mom in the bathroom and try to lightly broach the subject that it's midnight and

87

we're shopping at a gas station, but she cuts me off, asking if I needed to take a shower.

"What?" I ask.

"They have showers here," she explains.

"No, mom! Why would you ever think I would do that?"

"Just asking."

OK, suspicions confirmed.

When I tell them I'll be in the car, my dad looks disappointed that I don't want anything. I've talked before about the mystical powers catalogs hold over his prudent consumer behavior, but the Flying J is something else entirely. This seems to be like a religious pilgrimage for him. All of this crap somehow gains importance when shoved into a truck stop—ahem—Travel Plaza, and that I'm failing to take it in is upsetting him. I debate the lighter and settle on a coffee.

Sitting in the parking lot, I ask my parents to explain how the salute came to be. It turns out that on their first trip to Florida to scout out potential colleges for Ness, the muffler of our Suburban had been giving them problems. Afraid that the muffler might fall and drag against the road, potentially causing great harm, my father used a five dollar hacksaw to cut the muffler off of the car.

My dad is recounting the events of this story like a war hero narrating his memories of combat. "I pulled off to the side of the Interstate in the rain," he says. "The rain was ruthless. Cars zipped by at top speeds, just barely missing me, water everywhere. It was dangerous, Jessie! But if that muffler fell off out there in the rain while we were driving, someone could've been hurt. I knew what I had to do. I knew there was a small saw somewhere in the Suburban, so I searched for it, risked life and limb, and went out into the pouring rain to cut the muffler off the car. The rest of the trip was loud, but we made it home safely because of that saw."

"You cut the muffler off the Suburban?" I ask.

"I had to!"

"Can you even do that?!"

"Well, I did it. So the answer is yes. It can be done."

He pauses for a minute, like I'll need the time to digest the enormity of the tale. He turns in his seat to look at me. "That saw," he says thunderously, "was bought at a Flying J!"

I look at him without expression. "And?" I ask.

"Aaaaand," he says with exaggeration, "that's why we salute."

I wait for a second before saying anything. I want to launch into a speech about why his story makes no sense, but I stop myself. Martin Buber said, "All journeys have secret destinations of which the traveler is unaware." I always assumed the "secret destination" had to do with something spiritual, or within the self. But maybe he was talking about an actual place. Maybe Martin Buber was talking about arriving at unexpected destinations, like the Flying J. I knew we were driving down to Florida on this trip, and then driving back to New York, but I'm surprised to find myself at a truck stop in the middle of the night, laughing at my dad's story, and appreciating my parents' craziness. I'm thinking about it, and really, what's so horrible about a little salute and a story to go along with it? Yes, saluting a gas station is weird. And yes, cutting off a piece of your car with a tool bought where some people shower is unusual. But at least they're mindful of good fortune and sane enough to be thankful for it. I can salute that.

THEN THERE WERE THREE

Home from the road trip and settled back into our daily routines, it occurs to me that my *Groundhog Day* existence could very likely last forever. I've slipped back into my reclusive ways, only my oldest friend, the nap, left me after a rough falling out. Somewhere out on the open road I recognized that napping was a far too passive way to deal with my depression and panic attacks. So whenever I feel as though I'd like to nap, I go outside and mow the lawn. My perpetual melancholy has led to a perfectly manicured yard, and my father has never been happier. When he comes home for lunch to find me staring at the computer screen, he enthusiastically offers to bring the lawnmower over from the barn. In his world of mental health, a ride-on lawnmower is Zoloft, Vicodin, and Percocet all rolled into one, but better, because it has a blade deck.

My nap avoidance has created awkwardness around the house. Whenever I see a throw blanket on the sofa in mid-afternoon, I glance at it briefly, saying softly, "Oh... hello," and then slowly pass it by. There is a tension there and it's building up. Add to this living alone with my parents and it becomes a pretty intense series of time warps envisioned when I would normally be resting. Jumping ahead five years, the yard no longer has grass thanks to the three-a-day mows, I weigh nearly 300 pounds, wear sweatpants exclusively, and I own at least six of those semi-truck t-shirts, which, suddenly one day, seemed completely necessary.

Obviously it's unhealthy for a person like me to give up naps cold turkey. It'd be like a normal person giving up, I don't know, breathing. But I'm hoping the extra time spent in waking life will literally wake me up to my situation and push me into motion. So far it's only caused delirium and a few heart-to-heart talks with that throw blanket.

Because nine out of ten conversations I have throughout my day are either in my head or with bedding, I have very little to share when sitting down with my parents. Therefore, all dialogue and storytelling responsibilities are on their end. If the napping deficiency and evident lack of mental stability are not making it clear that I've hit a record new low, hearing my parents recount the events of their days helps turn that lens into focus.

The other night, my dad was describing a new man who came to work on the farm who for some reason doesn't talk. Dad went on to say that he has been miming out to the man how to perform various tasks around the farm. Acting out how to plant seeds, or imitating how one might pick up large rocks, my dad has essentially been training this man using charades.

After hearing him explain the situation, my mom asked, "Is he deaf, Steve? Or does he just not talk?

To which my dad replied, "Oh. I'm not sure."

So it's very likely for the past few weeks my father has led this man to believe they share the same problem.

My mother has been attending weekly TOPS meetings ("Taking Off Pounds Sensibly") and as a result we have to hear her talk about everything she eats and the effects it will have at weigh-in. "Oh, this tuna sub is good, but I'll probably be gaining a pound this week. Although, I did really well yesterday, so maybe I'll turtle."

I'm secretly fascinated by the TOPS meetings. The weigh-ins take place in the kitchen of a Methodist church and among chipped china and dish cloths there is a scale and two women who were nominated and elected to their positions. One elected official weighs the members while the other elected official records the weights in a journal. After everyone is told how they've done for the week, they move to the daycare center of the church and share the results with the group. If you lose weight, everyone claps twice. If you "turtle" (stay the same), everyone claps once. And if you gain weight, everyone says in unison, "We care." I particularly love this bit because the way my mother describes it is a monotone, lifeless, "We care." Plus, it has been my experience that when people say they care, they usually don't. I've taken this catch phrase on as my own because I think it's hilarious.

"Jess," my mom says, "The dishes need to be emptied."

"We care," I reply.

"I think it's time you took a job—any job," she'll say.

"We care," I'll reply.

It's wonderfully useful.

Living at home for so long is like watching the same movie over and over. I can anticipate certain scenes, I know what lines will be said—it's all predictable. Actually, it exceeds predictability. It's reciting the alphabet. It's something so well known that you almost forget what is being said. It's all just familiar sounds strung together with the same familiar rhythm. The daily conversations with my parents are the "L M N O P" portion of the alphabet. Say it enough times and it's just a gibberish noise that makes you lose focus for a few moments.

So what happens during our exchanges is that I'll say something, they'll say they couldn't understand me, I'll repeat it, they'll answer a different question entirely, and I'll resume my pained stare at the ceiling. Example:

Me: Do you have a TOPS meeting tonight?

Anticipated Response Thought Bubble: *You mumble.*

Mom: I'm sorry Jessica, I can't understand you when you mumble.

Thought: Try listening.

Me: Try listening.

Anticipated Response: *Please don't be rude.*

Mom: Please don't be rude.

Me: I'm sorry. Do you have a meeting at TOPS tonight?

Mom: I know, but they were two for $6 so I grabbed them.

Cue stare.

I think both Deb and Steve have had it with my blank stares. My contemplation exercises consist mainly of sitting on the sofa while staring at the floor, and I can understand why they'd find it upsetting. My mother is convinced I've slipped into an irreversible depression and keeps suggesting I get out of the house and "take a class."

"What class do you suggest I take?"

"I don't know, sign up for Jazzercise."

"Thank you for that. I'll do that immediately."

I'd actually love to see a Jazzercise class full of graduates living at home, confused about their life direction. Glum faces, attitudes bordering on pissed off, all slowly shuffling around with jazz hands. I think in lieu of placebos for anti-depression medications they should give patients t-shirts that read, "Who Feels Like Dancing?" If the drug companies don't go for it, those classes for graduates without jobs should pass them out.

My father has little to say about my daily routine of sitting and thinking but I can tell by the look on his face that he wants to say, "You know, those lawn aeration shoes are always just a phone call away."

It's Sunday morning and I can hear my parents making breakfast in the kitchen. Sunday is the one day of the week my father doesn't work so it's the three of us around the house all day, having the same confusing conversations, trying to understand each other over endless cups of coffee and the Sunday paper. I love my parents, and I love reading the newspaper. It's hard to love both at the same time.

Deb and Steve are the kind of people who need to share everything they read in the paper, the moment they read it. That's fine; I'm the same way when I come across something interesting. However, the two of them usually start out with the advertisement inserts and feel compelled to comment on random sales like they're hard-hitting news stories.

"Well, look at that!" my dad shouts. "There you go, boy! Harvest Oatmeal made with Martin Farms Butternut Squash! I'll tell you what!"

"That's actually in the news?" I ask.

"Well, it's in this Wegman's flyer," he says, handing me the page. "Look, they have the recipe and everything!"

"Oh, Steve, look at this," my mom says. "They took ten dollars off the price of that panini maker. Now that's a good deal."

It's their house and their paper. I have no right to ask them to be quiet for a minute while I finish reading an article. But I do anyway. "Sorry guys, can I just finish reading this?"

"Oh, sorry," my mom says, putting up her hands like she's interrupted a doctor in the middle of surgery.

I finish my article and shout out in protest, "Can you believe this with Bush?!"

"Jess, we're trying to read here," my mom says, mocking me. "Could you just be quiet for a minute?"

"You're reading coupons!" I say. "You need absolute silence for coupons?"

"Science fair coupons?" my dad asks.

"What? No, never mind," I say, defeated. Talking to them is like playing Telephone.

I read the three articles I can find concerning world news in our local paper and end up reading the *Miss Manners* and *Hints From Heloise* columns. I'm not a fan of either of them. If Miss Manners had any, she'd realize that talking in the third person is painfully annoying. And Heloise's hints are useless. A headline for her column one day read, "Don't Lay Eyeglasses Lenses Down." Thanks for the hint! In another column a reader suggested using the alarm on your cell phone as an alarm clock while traveling. Do you think it could work, Heloise? A clock as a clock? Here's a hint for Hel: You can't call it a hint if it's blatantly obvious.

I would love to take part in a scavenger hunt organized by Heloise.

Item 1: Find an old blue mitten

Hint: It's in my bedroom dresser, third drawer down, underneath the vibrating egg.

Local newspapers offer little help in solving my unemployment problem. For a while I was checking my daily horoscope for signs of progress but that proved to be a horrible idea. One day the Sagittarius reading said an answer I had been waiting for would come by two o'clock. Certain that it would be an employer I sat around waiting for a call until two in the afternoon. When nothing came I thought, of course, two in the morning! So I waited that out too until I realized I'm an idiot and stopped reading them.

I put the paper down and watch my dad as he makes his fourth Belgian waffle of the day. After eating breakfast out one morning a while ago, I mentioned that buying a waffle maker would pay for itself in one use, as opposed to paying $5 a piece at a diner. Working it out in his head, my father agreed and immediately went out to buy one. Since then, he has felt it is his fiscal responsibility to stuff his face with Belgian waffles nearly every Sunday morning.

"Aren't you going to make yourself sick?" I'll usually

ask.

"Just think of the savings!" he'll reply.

The man truly believes he is improving my family's financial situation by ingesting unnatural amounts of batter in a single sitting.

Once the waffle has reached crispy perfection, he asks if I'd care for it. "I'm getting a little full," he admits. Placing it on a plate and handing it to me he says, "That'll be five dollars please! No, I'm only kidding. But seriously, think of the savings!"

I thank him and take my breakfast to the living room.

"Oooh," he says, "Not in there, okay? Sticky sticky."

Growing up, my father would influence us to wash our hands by insisting they were sticky, as if we'd dipped them in molasses for an hour. I think he would have preferred that, due to some genetic mutation, we had all been born with candy apples for hands so that his arguments would have had some foundation.

I return to the island with my waffle and sit back down with my parents, retreating into my mind. It's a silent cerebral siesta I take on Sundays to a place where *One Note Samba* plays on repeat and where the things I say aren't misunderstood. Far away from discussions of electricity, the lawn, my plans to move, or the one-day sale at Target that is apparently above the fold news today. The dog's barks are muffled, my father's complaints muted, and a waffle has never tasted better.

****

My grandma's birthday is coming up and my mother and I have taken Amtrak down to Long Island to surprise her. If you've never had the pleasure, Amtrak leaves much to be desired. Every part of my being wants to support rail transportation but something about the lack of speed, the abundance of smells, and the food from the snack car, prohibits that. Whenever I take the train I find myself coming up with new slogans for the company based on my experiences during the ride. One time the train I was riding stopped on the tracks for about an hour before finally moving backwards. The slogan for that trip was, "Amtrak: Wait, This Way?" Another time while watching people board at Albany I overheard a man say, "Gah, this train smells like a bathroom." The slogan that time was, "Amtrak: Smells Like Bathroom." The slogans aren't really cryptic. Today, the man who gave us our tickets at the station in Rochester said without even the slightest hint of sarcasm, "Here are your tickets. The train leaves when it gets here." That should be their slogan, hands down. "Amtrak: It Leaves When It Gets Here."

This trip down to New York City went surprisingly well and with my faith in the American rail restored, we happily wheeled our luggage to the LIRR to catch a train out to Long Island. Making our way through Penn Station my mom commented on the genius behind wheeled luggage. "Gosh, this is a great idea! Wheeled luggage! It's just brilliant!"

Really, mom? Brilliant? How about Einstein and the few math problems he pieced together? What about Mozart? He seemed bright. But the guy who put the little wheels on the bag, he's tops in your book, huh?

Once out on Long Island, my cousin Jonathan picks us up at Hicksville station and we arrive at my grandma's house close to midnight. He had called her earlier that day saying he would be over late so that she wasn't completely shocked when someone knocked on her door in the middle of the night. Peering through the front window, my grandma screams when she sees us. She probably would have screamed even if she knew we were coming, but the noise seems to intensify the surprise.

Cutting her hellos short, she runs to her freezer saying, "I'll make chicken cutlets, you've got to be starving."

I'm telling you, lions.

"Grandma, don't cook," I say. "Let's go out and grab something to eat."

"Don't be silly," she says. "Nothing's open. It's fine."

My Uncle Greg, who lives with my grandma, comes into the kitchen and suggests that we go to an all-night diner. We pull the frozen chicken from her clenched hands and pile into my uncle's car. I should mention that my uncle has a penchant for doing voices and making noises. I've always felt a closeness to Robin Williams because essentially, he is my Uncle Greg. If Robin Williams enjoyed scrapbooking and photography, and lived with my grandma, he'd be my Uncle Greg. He has a vault of catchphrases that he's collected over the years and shouts them out at random times, making everyone laugh, following up with a noise made by shaping his mouth into an "o" and flicking his throat with his fingers. A typical family gathering usually includes hearing quotes from old movies or inside-jokes repeated incessantly, before listening to weird sound effects for an hour. He also used to chase us around when we were kids, wearing a Halloween mask and shouting, "SCALE!" threatening to stand on us if he caught us. I'd be lying if I said it didn't used to scare the shit out of me. I'm still 80% convinced that if given the opportunity, he would stand on me. But I digress.

Uncle Greg is at the wheel searching his presets for the most perfect "surprise visit late-night food run" tune. I must admit he comes close to perfection with the theme song from the 1987 film, *Mannequin*, "Nothing's Gonna Stop Us Now." Blasting it from the radio we all sing along, except my grandma, who is too busy shooting her arms in the air, dangerously close to my face, shouting, "Yay!" Uncle Greg belts out impromptu lyrics incorporating his noises into the song as passengers in other cars look over to see what is going on.

As I often do in times like these—which seem to happen more often than I'd like to disclose—I draw myself far out of the situation in slow-motion and observe it like a person hiding behind a newspaper, or anyone unrelated to the chaos: A group of people singing the theme from *Mannequin* stop at a red light in the middle of the night as their car bounces up and down. The middle-aged man driving seems to be playing an air trumpet while the middle-aged woman riding shotgun is doing the robot. There is an older woman in the back seat who appears to be punching two young adults in the head.

But trying to analyze the situation as an outsider can only last for so long. This moment is my life. This car of singing crazies is my family. And whether it's from behind a newspaper or right next to me, I see it. So I sing along, trying not to get hit by my grandma's shooting arms and contentedly await my late-night falafel.

A few days later, thanks to the chicken cutlet sandwiches that my grandma eventually makes us anyway, our return trip on the train is made more manageable sans snack car. When my father meets us at the station he helps with the bags and we make our way to the car. Rolling the luggage through the parking lot he turns to me and says, "These rolling suitcases are great, right? Jess, you're smart, you could think of something like this!" His comment makes me realize how perfect my parents are for each other. Both of them had taken the time to consider the genius behind wheeled luggage. That's just written in the stars right there. Plus, it's nice to know my parents have so much faith in my abilities. I'm smart, I could figure out something else to put wheels on.

Once at home, my mother runs to her bathroom scale. A trip to my grandmother's involves almost constant eating—it's a medical mystery how it's possible. From the bathroom I can hear her yell, "I turtled! I can't believe I turtled!"

In the living room, even though no one is around to appreciate it, I clap once.

SEARCH FOR MEANING

The questions I asked so often as a child seemed extremely important back then. "What's the deal with needing to ask the lunch ladies permission to throw away my trash?" "How come I always have to be Luigi when we play Nintendo?" "Why can't I have a RonCo Electric Food Dehydrator?" That last one always came up around my birthday or before Christmas when my mother would so cleverly ask, "What would you like this year besides a food dehydrator?" I don't know why she was so hell-bent on not letting me have one. Those conversations always ended with me shouting, "You make your own fruit roll-ups! What don't you understand?!" before running to my room.

All those childhood queries were probably the significant questions in life, but over time I was tricked into thinking otherwise by society, my philosophy classes, and every author in the self-help section at Barnes and Noble. As I grew older, a recurring theme I kept noticing was that asking larger questions seemed to be the key to understanding larger concepts. Why do we exist? What is our essence? What does it mean to have meaning? But tossing out those kinds of questions around an impressionable young girl, namely me, the Queen of Indecision and heir to the throne of "I don't know," was bound to cause confusion at some point.

My unemployment and introspective tendencies have created a Petri dish of contemplation. I'm inside my head waiting for answers to grow, only to find a rapidly expanding blob of questions about what constitutes a meaningful life. I suppose that's what happens during transition periods or in moments when a life we knew starts to crumble. We all look for something bigger than ourselves to help make sense of what we can't explain. When life is messy we ask sweeping questions about our own importance. When life moves along smoothly we tend to focus on things like food dehydrators.

There is no doubt my unemployment is causing me to question my own value. It seems many people find their meaning through their work. I know this because I hear them talk about it all the time, lacing their conversations with words like "rewarding" and "fulfilling." Telling a girl who can't find a job how great jobs are is not helpful. It's like those couples who amp up their PDA around their single friends. Who does that?

The problem is that I never had a profession in mind when people talked about the future. Outside of make-believe, career goals weren't given much thought. When we were little, Nessa and I used to dress up in my father's suits and have my mom make our lunches, asking her not to say a word. She'd take our orders and we'd get to business nursing a scotch on the rocks (apple juice, extra ice) because that seemed like a business drink. I was Jim and Nessa was Ed, although at other times she also went by Drew McAlister. It never occurred to me to have a last name. I was just one of those elusive businessmen too busy for formal introductions. Years later my mother found a JC Penny credit card with the name Drew McAlister scribbled on the back and she asked, "Who is Drew McAlister?" Without hesitation Nessa simply answered, "Oh, that's me."

We also recently found an old check for $100 made out to Cook County Hospital signed by Drew McAlister. The memo said, "For Lunch."

But anyway, dressed up as Jim and Ed, talking business, we'd order from our mom, who acted interested and said that she was serving a lunch special of sandwiches and soup. After the food was served we just wanted her to disappear but she'd always pry.

"So Jim, how's business?"

"Mom!"

"I'm not your mom! M'name's Peggy. I run this little place."

"Mom!"

"I told you, call me Peggy."

"Please leave!"

"Well it turns out I have to go to the stock room anyway. Big party coming in for dinner tonight."

"Leave!"

"I hope this attitude won't be reflected in my tip."

And she'd walk away.

"Sorry about that, Ed. So, as I was saying…"

For a seven-year-old I think I had a pretty good feel for the business world. Lots of papers were essential in that it gave the illusion of lots of business and lots of ideas. Also it was good to carry about fifteen pens, just in case. I always picked up the bill, which consisted of asking Peggy to put it on my tab, and after getting a dry erase board for my birthday I was sure to bring it to every meeting. Though I never got around to defining what it was I did for a living, graphs were a big part of it. And so it would go for hours—seriously. Often after the meetings we would both have to catch a train, which involved sitting on the living room sofas, still in my father's suits. If we watched TV or put in a video, it wasn't enough to disrupt our suspended disbelief of the train ride.

It wasn't until I was in middle school that my lack

of career path planning became evident to me. I remember sitting in a Home and Careers class learning the average salaries of jobs in which I had no interest before finally raising my hand to ask what else there was. Unsure of what I meant, my teacher asked if I wanted her to Xerox a different career chart for me. I explained that that wasn't my point and tried to make myself clear.

"What if all I want to do is travel around and occasionally stop to meet up with friends and family?" I asked.

"Well then," she replied, handing me three new charts, "perhaps you'd be interested in an occupation with the armed forces."

She had completely misunderstood. Failing to grasp that maybe I never wanted a job, my teacher went on to say that careers give people direction, a sense of purpose. And there it was. *Purpose.* The word fell like a cartoon anvil. It hurled downward complete with whistle noise while I waited with a helpless expression for it to reach me. *Purpose.* It hit hard, flattening me into my desk chair as the symbolic stars and birds circled around my head. If careers gave people a sense of purpose, what did it say about me that I might not want a career? What was I supposed to know about purpose anyway? Besides showing up to classes like Home and Careers, did I even have one? I was convinced that I did and despite the Xeroxed pie chart wisdom handed to me by Ms. Kreitz, I didn't think I needed a job to find it.

I started looking everywhere. I listened and watched everything twice as carefully, hoping to gain some insight as to what that teacher meant by purpose. After paying heed to the prophetic words of my main musical influences of the time, I only learned that just in case one was not aware, Miami was in fact, on the scene, and also, because Tag Team was back again, whoomp, there it was. But I wasn't discouraged. I felt that maybe if I could find a common purpose in others it would lead me to my own. The idea of recognizing a universal of human nature has been present within me from about this period of time. People-watching was promoted from favorite airport pastime to the greatest opportunity for truth-seeking I-Spy. Before any flight we ever took, my sisters and I used to give strangers names and stories as they passed by because it was the most entertaining way to kill time while sitting in one place.

"This is Thomas. He's off to Dallas to meet his high school sweetheart at their twenty year reunion. He's told himself that if she comes alone again this time he'll tell her he loves her."

"This is Chip. He's a pilot who started to fly as a way to get over his fear of heights. On the whole, Chip is not a happy man."

"This family is the Wilsons. They're off to Hawaii even though Mrs. Wilson hates warm weather. She's determined to take a family picture on the beach and use it for the cover of the annual Wilson Newsletter that tells people what they've been up to even though no one cares. Mrs. Wilson will end up getting an awful sunburn and the picture won't be used."

Prior to being confronted with ideas of purpose or meaning, people-watching just seemed like a simple game to play. However, I eventually realized the unifying strength it held. When we give strangers names and stories, we've connected to them, in some bizarre way that is based on untruths, but still. Sure, I don't know you, and your name is most likely not Ingrid, and you're probably not the inventor of Brown Sugar and Cinnamon Pop Tarts, but I've found something in five seconds of you that I find in myself, and that's what makes us human. Biologists and anthropologists might say that this is not what makes us human, I'm sure there're other more defining reasons, but I think it's key to our humanity—not the Pop Tarts, just realizing that we're all folks. We're all here. Observing crowds and groups of people affords me the chance to make grand sweeping statements about the human condition. Even if these are juvenile observations, I still feel like I'm getting closer to discovering something about myself by noticing universal things about everyone else.

Examples include:

—People like to hear laughs. If people hear a warm, genuine laugh, they are usually inclined to turn and smile, because for the most part, the sound of another person's laughter is enjoyable to hear.

—People like to be offered gum. Even if they don't want any, or don't like gum, it's nice to be asked. People just appreciate the invitation to chew some gum.

—People love to talk about their mouths. I truly believe that the only cure for biting your tongue is to say, "Ow, I just bit my tongue." As soon as people bite their tongues or have a canker sore, or their tooth hurts, they want to tell everyone they see about it. I don't know why, it's just how it is. Other ailments are often far too personal or embarrassing to bring up in casual conversation, but people are more than willing to share with an acquaintance what's going on in their mouths.

But even after establishing these things, I've always had a nagging feeling that there must be something deeper; that my search for a human nature universal should go beyond observations about gum. In school we were taught to peel away at everything in front of us, looking for hidden meaning. It was usually in English classes that we ripped texts apart searching for metaphor and symbolism. Although, once in an American history class we talked about *The Wizard of Oz* as a metaphor for William Jennings Bryan's "Cross of Gold" speech. That can't count though because *The Wizard of Oz* could be a metaphor for anything. That's what makes it so timeless. That, and people love to watch little people sing about lollipops—another universal. But I digress.

It was in my senior year of high school that I finally became fed up with the use of metaphor as a means of finding meaning. Just once, I thought to myself, could something normal, maybe even something boring, be the source of meaning? And if it couldn't, could we stop turning it into a metaphor in order to make it appear meaningful?

I remember sitting in my English class during our poetry unit as the teacher passed out copies of the poem we would be reading and analyzing that day. It was called "The Flying Goose" or something like that. It described the way the goose looked, it's surroundings, how the goose flew through the air, and how it related to nature. All in all, not a bad little poem about a goose.

When we finished reading it and my teacher asked for interpretations. I was surprised when so many hands shot up at once. "Wow," I said to myself, "these people must really like geese." The first kid to react to the poem offered that the goose represented a homeless man. I waited for him to say he was just kidding but instead he continued with his interpretation using lines from the poem. I could be making this up, but I think I remember him saying something about how the sky was a shopping cart. Anyway, I waited for him to finish so the teacher could tell him he was off the mark, but nothing. Instead the teacher nodded slowly and thanked him for his refreshing view. Hmm, OK.

I looked around the class to see how many other people were holding back bursts of laughter only to find everyone else nodding slowly with tilted heads. This couldn't be for real. Another girl went on to suggest that the goose represented a Third World country, and the girl sitting next to her thought it was an allegory for anorexia. I felt overwhelmed with confusion. But still, I looked around and saw people writing notes on their poems. I quickly reread the poem thinking, *I'm not crazy, right? The goose in this poem is a goose.* After reading all about the bird for a second time, confident I was not crazy, I wanted to cup my hands over my mouth and scream out to the class, "It's a goose, you idiots! It's about a flying goose! The poem is called THE FLYING

GOOSE! It's a goose!!!" But I didn't. I just waited quietly and hoped my teacher wouldn't ask me for an interpretation, forcing me to say it was a poem about psoriasis.

I think I knew at this point that I'd always be plagued with the search for meaning. The problem is, where do you draw the line between establishing something real and sounding completely foolish? That day in English has stuck out in my mind for all these years in that it helps remind me that sometimes, things just are.

When I studied in London I went to the Tate Modern quite often and for fun, I'd play, "Modern Artist vs. Realist." The rules are simple. For each piece of art you view, you describe it as the modern artist who created it, and a realist. Whoever has the more compelling argument wins.

Example:

Modern Artist: I created this as a commentary on communication and the bonds we create in contemporary society. The lack of life on either side of the line represents our abandonment, both of others, and ourselves. We're too busy to take these calls, but the bright light shinning above us is the call from a higher power, a spiritual calling if you will, beseeching us to reach out to others. By taking the call, we justify the existence of others and in turn, justify our own existence.

Realist: I see two tin cups connected by string. And the light isn't part of the exhibit, it's so the museum isn't dark.

The Realist almost always wins. Even if the Modern Artist has a truly interesting suggestion, it sounds ridiculous when the Realist describes what's actually there-- a blank canvas, toothbrushes, video of people smearing ketchup on themselves, golf balls. If you see human struggle or the meaning of life in these things, you're either lying or have paid way too much for higher education.

I'm not blind to the fact that all this contemplating I've been doing lately is an idle time luxury. On the contrary,

I'm fully aware of it. Knowing what I must sound like as I try to make sense of my situation has created a thick layer of guilt and annoyance that floats atop my inwardness like heavy cream. But when you spend your entire life studying, cramming, writing, and reading, thinking that it will all lead up to a single goal, you become disillusioned when you realize you never actually knew what the goal was. And maybe that disillusionment is the point; it reminds us not to rely too heavily on the search for meaning. Maybe our meaning can be summed up by the Law of Parsimony, which states, "When multiple explanations exist, the simplest is usually true." That we'll know what holds meaning for us when we find ourselves smiling about it at random times. Perhaps our search doesn't have to be anything deeper than that. Trying too hard to describe our purpose with metaphors we don't even understand may prove to do little good. Considering what things could be, or how things could be, is important, don't get me wrong, but sometimes we just have to recognize things for exactly what they are. If you can see a moment, or situation, or a period of time in your life for what it is, and find value there, I think you're doing alright. Or maybe the goose is anorexic, I don't know.

OPEN-EYED SNEEZE

With my introspective tendencies heightened exponentially by living with my parents, thinking has become the primary activity on my daily schedule. Swimming is penciled in right after my 1:30 Thought Session and right before my 2:30 Advanced Thought For Unemployed Thinkers, but we don't have a pool so I usually just eat during that gap.

It's hard to listen to myself think when Deb and Steve ask me every five minutes, "What are you thinking about?" Readers have the luxury of the book as a defense of sorts, a wall between them and the outside world. So even if people ask them what they're reading, they can just flash the title and raise the book-wall back to their face. Thinkers have no such wall. They just sit there, sometimes with concerned looks, and anyone who happens to pass by has the option to ask what's on their mind. Thoreau must have run into this problem before heading off to Walden. Just on the verge of something profound, some guy asked him why he looked so serious and he stood up in protest and said, "That's it! I'm moving to the woods!"

I'm spending the day at a beach on Lake Ontario. It's not too far from my house and I figure it'll be easier to think here without being interrupted by my mother's comments about my think tank for one. "Jess, are you going into your think tank again? If you are, could you clean the water? Do you need a filter for that tank? Maybe one of those little treasure chests to put at the bottom? Do they sell those for think tanks?"

It'll be nicer to think to myself by myself.

If you ever want to feel alone, go to an upstate New York beach on an autumn Wednesday. There were three cars in the parking lot when I got here. Being alone on a beach is good for thought. It makes you listen to your wandering mind. I'm looking at Lake Ontario, pleased with the day, just sort of letting my head unwind.

It's been difficult these past months to sit back and do nothing while everyone around me moves. My head feels cloudy because of it. Some of my friends from high school are married and having babies. Babies! I don't even like to carry a purse. And if they're not starting families they're off in grad school getting more degrees, or in New York City finding exciting jobs, while I'm caught in a daze watching it all pass by around me. I seem to be paralyzed in this isolated people-watching session, observing my peers go off and live while I listen to my dad talk about the expired milk he used for his oatmeal this morning. "No need to thank me. I hope you enjoyed your fresh milk." The detrimental side of boredom is that it allows too much time to look at those moving around us instead of realizing the incredible force with which we ourselves are moving.

There was a physics problem that fascinated me as an eighth grader. It asked: If a person flying on a plane stood up and jumped during the flight, would he move back a little in the aisle by the time his feet came back down to the floor? I remember staring at the problem, wanting to fly somewhere immediately and test it for myself. Eventually I found out. On a flight to Europe I stood up in the aisle making sure no one was looking. I jumped up and fell but wasn't sure if it was the force of the plane that had done it or jumping dangerously close to a seat. By the third attempt a man asked me what I was doing and I explained the physics problem to him. He said that he was an engineering professor and that the answer was no. I wouldn't move back after jumping because I was traveling at the same rate as the airplane. I thanked him and sat back down, amazed.

All those years I'd flown I'd never realized I was moving so fast—the plane, obviously, but not me. We too often overlook the power of whatever it is we're a part of, seeing only others and not ourselves as a portion of a greater force in motion.

I love watching people do paperwork on planes. How busy must they be to move at 600 mph and still have work to be done? Their hectic lives seem to have more importance than mine. I never do anything on a plane. I'm the type of person who fully examines the safety card. Not because I'm particularly interested in what to do in an emergency situation, but because I like to make up stories about the cartoon people in the pamphlet.

This is Maria. She was on a flight home to visit her mother, Rosa, who is in the hospital recovering from a gardening accident, when all of a sudden there was some turbulence. The plane came to a rough landing but she escaped with the help of the crew and this inflatable slide. She lost her shoes during the evacuation but remembered her mother didn't like that pair anyway so all was well. For the inconvenience, the airline gave her two round-trip tickets anywhere in the continental United States. She plans on taking her mother—who has always had a strange fascination with large curved pieces of metal, hence the gardening accident—to St. Louis to see the famous arch.

But after learning that everyone on a plane moves at the same rate, I was overwhelmed with relief. Being overwhelmed with relief is strangely exhausting. It's like sitting on a massage chair at Brookstone or finding that perfect spot in your ear with a Q-tip. You become aware of how relaxed you can be. Understanding that we're moving individually and together with such momentum frees us from worrying about taking jumps. The floor won't move out from beneath you, bringing you further back from where you started, because life and your life are moving at equal velocities. It's sort of huge.

Accepting this involuntary movement was particularly hard for me to do. On long car trips Vanessa and I used to play games of increasing levels of annoyance. There was "Mr. Pillowhead" in which players would put a pillow over their face and speak in Cockney accents similar to the "Ello, Gov'nah" chimney sweep.

"I'm Mistah Pillow-ed."

"No, I'm Mistah Pillow-ed."

The conversation continued until someone couldn't breathe and then they lost. It was no *Travel Pop-o-Matic Trouble*, but it passed the time.

Other games included "I'm Not Touching You," "Hot Hands," and "Made you Flinch," which were all based on testing each other's reflexes. I have no idea what we were trying to prove. We must have thought we were cool for being able to limit eye blinks. All I know is that I didn't like the idea of someone controlling my movement. Like when the doctor would hit my knee with the little rubber mallet. I hated that. I used to hold my leg as tightly as I could against the back of the table.

"OK," the doctor would say. "I'm just going to need you to relax your leg."

And when he hit it there would be a slight delay before I kicked my leg up as far as it could go.

"OK," the doctor said again. "Just relax the leg. Let it move naturally."

Right, because hitting my leg with random objects is natural. I'm not a puppet, doc. You want to see it move, I'll kick this leg for an hour, but you and your mallet aren't going to make me dance.

I was full of such an untrusting rage, believing that doctors held conventions to discuss new ways to hit patients and make limbs jerk out in a comical manner. So I took those car games seriously. "Made You Flinch" was my preventative training camp for looking like a fool. Flick your finger near my eye, fake-throw a ball at me, I'm not flinching. By ten I had conditioned myself to appear unaffected by nearly everything around me and it was almost a source of satisfaction for me. It wasn't until I heard about open-eyed sneezes that I realized the complete ridiculousness of my silent pride.

During a lunch conversation in grade school, a friend mentioned that sneezing with your eyes open was impossible. Others agreed that they'd heard the same thing. Convinced that these slackers just lacked the dedication to games of reflex, I used every sneeze as an opportunity to prove them wrong. This took an arsenal of patience because unless you have allergies or sniff pepper—which I debated trying—you basically have to wait around for it. But when that tingle in my nose came, I steeled myself and propped my eyes open with thumb and forefinger. Besides poking yourself in the eye, sneezing on your clothes, and looking like a moron, there's an intrinsic voice that tells you you're not so bright to continue this venture. After countless attempts, I finally gave up. My friends had been right. The open-eyed sneeze was not possible.

Reflecting back on it now, it was pretty absurd to try to force something so unnatural, to try to control the involuntary. I've been thinking a lot about involuntary things lately. Not just uncontrollable sneezes, but larger involuntary parts our lives, such as who we are. Aristotle said the causes of nature—the matter, the form, what initiates motion, and what something is for—often amount to one. That what something is, and what it is for, are the same. He used the example of man generating man, and things in motion initiating motion. So perhaps to recognize what you are in terms of your passions or strengths is to know what you are for. And I'm so over answering Margot that I don't even think this applies exclusively to career goals. Mad-Lib it, fill in the blanks. Know what you are for in terms of relating to others, know what you are for yourself, whatever. I have to keep reminding myself that we each hold within us the foundation for our greatest natural self. When we stop fighting our own natural talents, or characteristics, or thoughts, we have nothing left to do but grow into form.

In *Physics II*, Aristotle talked about this idea of growing into form. He defined nature as that which has within itself a principle of change and stability, and said that natural things have an innate impulse to change. There's a comfort there. The comfort lies in the fact that we can take any shape we want while knowing that who we are on a fundamental level will always be. If what we are made of dictates our natural form, then maybe without even knowing it, we are constantly helping ourselves develop into what we should be. It's like Antiphon's Theory, which states that if we were to bury a bed, and the remains were able to sprout and grow, the result would not be a bed, but rather wood, because that is its natural form. We all have an innate impulse to change while knowing that we also possess the stability of a constant self. The latter is built-in reassurance for any unknown.

I'm a farm girl so I know that fields need fallow time. People are no different. I truly believe that, at some point, everyone must experience this unsown time that I've been experiencing lately so as to return to something clear and simple, something they can know for sure. Finding yourself in that place grants you the footing for steps into the uncertain, which is basically all of life. Eventually, all of our voluntary actions, our planning, and our hard work, will meet up with the involuntary, which is who we are intrinsically, and the particulars will reveal themselves.

It's important to start with what we know, with

things like coming home or being with family, but to remain there is to deny that necessary motion and change. By forcing the unnatural we create the absurd, and it's nearly impossible to find meaning in the absurd. At least, that's the thesis I've worked out in my head so far.

A group of seagulls has gathered around me, wrongly assuming that I have food to throw at them. Humans really screwed with the food chain when they decided to start feeding seagulls at the beach. I'm guessing gulls ate from the sea before figuring out they could get free chips by hanging around people. One of the seagulls is staring right at me like he hopes to intimidate a snack out of me, but even if I fed seagulls, which I don't, I have no food at the moment so this bird is out of luck. I stare back at him sort of shaking my head, trying to convey that I have nothing for him. He stares back. Looking at him, I notice that he only has one leg. I don't think I've ever seen that before. He looks kind of cute balancing on his one little leg. The bird gives me a look that says, "Why don't you take a picture?" but I realize birds probably don't think like that so I just keep staring.

Out of the corner of my eye I see a man walking the beach behind me so I turn to smile and we both say hello. Why is it we become friendlier when fewer people are around? He slows his pace and starts talking about the nice day. I point to the seagull I've been watching and ask the man if he's ever seen anything like that before.

"Have you ever seen that? A bird with just one leg?"

He considers the bird for a second before replying, "What do you need two legs for if you can fly?"

"Well," I say, "I suppose it limits footwear choices, but then, those aren't really feet, so." (I hate small talk. Hate it.)

He smiles softly and raises his eyebrows as if to say I've missed something important. We tell each other to enjoy the day and I turn back to look at the bird, waiting for the man to walk away.

Driving home from the lake I think about his comment, despite my best efforts not to do so. It sounded too much like something people would cross-stitch onto a pillow or use as the text on a poster of a one-legged seagull and a kitten. I have a bit of trouble accepting tidy phrases of wisdom because they usually lack practical application to messy life problems. But maybe that's too cynical. Words are powerful. And driving through country roads, surrounded by the natural, I begin to think the man might have had a point. Yes, he probably writes sayings for bookmarks for a living, but he had a point nonetheless. Birds should fly. Who cares about their legs?

Passing some of the fields of my father's farm I'm reminded that fall is moving in all around us. My dad's dedication to his work always comes to a forefront during this time of year. For all its beauty, fall is a season to be reckoned with. In its last defiant attempts to go out in glory before the shushing of winter arrives, fall can break a farmer's heart.

The changing leaves and noticeable crispness in the air are enough to divert the attention of most, but farmers know better. Fall rain and cold nights can be swords to your side in attempts to finish harvesting. The planting season is difficult but the fall harvest is the marriage of hard work and reward so it's something a bit more powerful.

I suppose to call it hard work is an extreme understatement. If you know a farmer you know it's more a way of life for them than anything else. Their lives are invested in the land, the earth. It's a connection to something so much bigger than they are that moves it leagues beyond job satisfaction. Farming for farmers is complete contentment in knowing what you're for. It's what Tennyson referred to as "the gleam:" pursuing that thing to which your heart goes out. And I see that in my dad every autumn. This year, strangely, I'm jealous of it.

As kids, his job made almost no sense to us. The long hours, coming home exhausted, knowing what you'd be doing the same time next year. To me, he was basically the personification of that machine that resets the pins at a bowling alley.

Sometimes on nights when he had to go to bed early so as to wake up early, we'd ask if he'd ever thought of doing something else. He'd pause for a second before saying no, and then go into his room. Minutes later he would come back out into the living room dressed in a football jersey, calling out plays, saying that maybe he would have wanted to be in the NFL. We'd laugh and he'd say goodnight and go back into his room. Minutes later he'd come out wearing a suit and tie saying that maybe he could have been a businessman working in an office, and he'd walk quickly around the living room looking to his wrist checking the fake time on an imaginary watch and we'd laugh some more. It was an impromptu Halloween of various lives that he could have led.

This would go on for about an hour — seriously. He'd come back out to the living room wearing any makeshift outfit he could find, making up songs for some jobs, funny voices for others. We simply thought he was just trying to make us smile every time he did this. And even if that's all it was, it helped reaffirm that his job suited him so well. We really couldn't see him as we knew him until he finally came out one last time in his pajamas and said he had to get to sleep for an early day. My mom hated when he did this because she always walked into their room to find a huge pile of clothes and hats on the floor.

If the idea is to grow into form starting with the sense of self that I already know, then maybe home is the most appropriate place for me to do that. Perhaps my parents' suggestions of a chicken place, or Riverdance, or Mars were all just funny outfit changes to remind me of my most natural fit. And even though I'm still not entirely sure what that natural fit might be, I'm oddly relaxed about it. I'm starting to feel like that's just something that will come.

Jess Martin

Wanting to jump into a fully realized version of myself or trying to force what I will become instead of focusing on who I am, is just as ridiculous as focusing on a bird's missing leg, or trying to sneeze with open eyes.

PORTRAIT OF A NIGHTSTAND

I'm moving to San Francisco. Well, not really. I've been thinking about moving to San Francisco. It just helps my decision process to say it definitively like that. I am moving to San Francisco. Repeating it like a daily affirmation softens the blow of actuality when I remember that I've never even been to San Francisco, I know very little about the city, and I have nothing to do once I get there. But I am moving to San Francisco, so I guess I'll have to figure all that stuff out when I arrive.

Despite what my sisters say, it has little to do with *Full House*, but I'd be lying if I said it didn't play some minor role. During the whole "WWJD" craze, I seriously debated making "What Would Kimmy Gibbler Do?" wristbands, but thought I might run into problems with royalties so I didn't.

But here's what happened: The other night while my mother was burning the chicken she was attempting to pan-sear, the kitchen and most of the house was engulfed in a lemon-herb smoke cloud. This, of course, made the dogs go crazy with every inhale and they were barking beyond control as my mom stood near the stove waving at the pan, as if an enthusiastic goodbye might help the smoke to get the hint that it was time to go.

During this commotion, the phone rang. Choking through my hello, the caller introduced himself and asked to speak with me concerning a part-time editing job for which I had applied. With eyes watering from chicken smoke, I quickly tried to remember what job he was talking about. I couldn't, so I did the most logical thing—I faked it.

"Yes, of course. Thanks for getting in touch with me." I said as I squeezed my eyes shut to avoid the smoke and snapped at the dogs to stop barking.

"No problem. I was wondering if we could meet and talk a little bit about the project."

"That'd be great. I could meet you sometime later this week, does that work for you?"

"Actually, it's a short-term gig, I just basically need someone to log footage. Would you be able to meet tomorrow?"

"Right. Tomorrow. Remind me again where you're located?"

"Do you need directions? Are you coming from San Francisco or do you live in the East Bay?"

[Shit.]

I went on to explain that I was currently living in New York and could fly out immediately, but he said it wouldn't be worth it because of the short timeline for the project.

I hung up and explained to my mother that I might have just had my first official phone interview. And even though it was horribly unsuccessful, San Francisco had a nice ring to it. San Francisco. A city name with a rhythm. "Are you coming from San Francisco?" "Yes, I live in San Francisco." And thus, the idea to move was planted.

I suppose my chronic reading problem might have played a role in this sudden decision to move as well. I've noticed that many of the authors I enjoy reading live there so I figure the city must be on to something. I know nothing of writers except for what films make of them, but it seems that wherever they choose to settle would probably be quite nice. Movies always show writers working for five solid minutes before going off to meet friends for dinner, or stopping to do anything else besides write. That lifestyle appeals to me on about a thousand different levels. San Francisco most likely has tons of great restaurants and bars because nothing helps the creative process quite like good food and lots of beer. And if you think of writers as working from home, their homes would probably be comfortable and in neighborhoods conducive to thought. A city full of nice areas for walks to clear the mind, and various coffee shops to stop for brainstorming breaks. That's the picture I've painted in my head of the city I've never seen: Lots of people eating and drinking, walking around with journals or laptops, stopping occasionally to write books. That's good enough for me.

It's such an American start for an East-Coaster to go west because the idea offers a chance for immediate change. Even if nothing happens, something happens. I think I need California and its promise of adventure. I need the West and its ideas of freedom. But mostly, I need to get out of my parents' house, because honestly, if I'm asked to mow the lawn one more time I'm going to set the machine on fire.

When I first share the idea about San Francisco with my parents, it's met with some resistance. My dad is all for it, but feels I should find employment before leaving. He seems to be missing that that's what I've been trying to do since May. My mother doesn't quite understand the city choice and my explanation of liking the work of writers who live there does little to solidify my position in her mind. She asks, "So because you liked a Dave Eggers book you want to fly across the country?"

I know she didn't say it with the intent to discourage me, but I really wish she hadn't sown that seed of reality into my newly sprouting idea garden. I'm the poster child, spokesperson, President, and member of the Over-

Examined Life Club and the fastest way for me to change my mind is to hear a point that I can't refute. What am I thinking? Basing my decision to move to an unfamiliar city on a few good books and a TGIF sitcom is not exactly a well-rounded plan.

Screw it. For the first time in a long time, I've decided to stop thinking and just go. The biggest decisions are as simple and as difficult as that. Just going. Just doing something. Once you get there you always think, "Oh, that was easy." It's just a matter of doing it. The hardest part of working out is getting dressed for the gym, right?

Finding a super ridiculously cheap flight to SF, I book it and start scouring Craigslist for potential roommates. I'll have four days to explore the city, narrow down a neighborhood I like, meet a chill roommate, and sign a lease. No problem.

Looking for a roommate in college is easy; you just ask your friends. And the first year of school, they give you one. Even though you don't know your first roommate, you know you have things in common. You're about the same age, you both finished high school, you go to the same college, you both download music illegally, etc. But looking for a roommate after college on Craigslist is like walking down a city street and randomly selecting someone to split utilities with.

"Excuse me, sir. I know we don't know each other, but do you like to keep your common area living space tidy? And if so, would you like to share an apartment together?"

There are a lot of weirdos out there who need roommates and you know nothing about them. We were indoctrinated since childhood about "stranger danger" only to grow up and be told to search for them under the Rooms/Shared link and try to move in with them.

—But I don't know them.

—Yeah, but you really can't afford to live by yourself, so it's OK.

—So the whole candy thing and avoiding vans? Forget about that?

—No, you should remember those, but you can totally share a stranger's toilet if it cuts your rent in half.

To be honest, the apartment hunt is just as daunting as the job hunt. Going through each listing, I try to envision the living dynamic with different types of roommates. Do I want to live with militant lesbians in San Francisco, or is that too much of a cliché? Do I want to live with students? One roommate? Two roommates? Do they have a dog? Hardwood floors? Hot water included? Do I want to live rent-free? Because that's possible too, according to one ad. All I have to do is be comfortable with my potential roommate's nudist lifestyle and occasionally clean the apartment naked. Right. Anything that I'd save in rent I'd end up spending on towels. "Um, could you not sit there, roomie? Thanks."

Another apartment listing said only, "I have gluten allergies. Please also have gluten allergies." It left a little to be desired in terms of actual housing info.

And some ads are so specific I feel like I will never find a place.

```
Vegan household seeks environ-
mentally-conscious full-time em-
ployee with volunteer experience
to share room in 4-bedroom house.
An interest in composting is a
plus.
```

Next! Frankly, I don't want a living situation where I have to constantly ask, "What do I do with this?" before throwing something away. "Sorry guys, I forget. Do we bury apple cores or should I just eat it?"

```
Roommate will be gainfully em-
```

```
ployed, not watch endless hours
of TV, and will have her own life.
```

Um, maybe on opposite day.

```
Housing    references    needed,
last five months pay stubs, first,
last, plus two-month security de-
posit required.
```

Right. I'm pretty sure I'll be borrowing money from my grandma for this move but I'm not about to ask her for $3,000. Would it be cool if I just had my grandma call you and tell you how much she loves me? Also, what's a pay stub? Does that have something to do with a payday? And if so, could you tell me a little more about that, please? It's been awhile.

After reading enough of these ads, all of my job-search insecurities come out to play and I'm left searching through used bike postings instead.

It's such a tricky little circle. It's a revolving door that I'd so gladly use if I could just figure out how to jump in. I need to live in a city to get a job there, to pay for rent for the apartment that I can't get a room in because I love to watch TV and don't know how to recycle eggshells.

I end up emailing an artist in Nob Hill who has an extra bedroom and I figure I can look for other places once I arrive.

A few days later, my parents drive me to the airport for the requisite elongated goodbye, complete with tears (despite the fact that I've booked a roundtrip ticket) and the forcing of spare change and five-dollar bills into my coat pocket. As my dad shoves the money at me, he makes suggestions for its use. "For coffee." "For a paper." "For a beer." We say one final goodbye and I head to my gate.

Waiting on the plane for the remaining passengers

to board, I crack open a fresh journal to document the moment.

> *En Route To San Francisco:*
>
> *Beginnings are always hardest. Much harder than endings. Don't get me wrong, endings are difficult, often full of unfulfilled wishes, but the fact that we have time to prepare for these moments must allow us to see that despite all the struggles that come with endings, they are never as hard as the start. The difficult part about endings is that we break away from the familiar, but that to which we have grown accustomed was once unknown, and there are few things as terrifying as the unknown. Endings allow for reflection whereas beginnings call for projection. There are too many variables to make this an effortless task and a study of time will demonstrate to the student the difficulties of assigning specifics to the future. So this is where I find myself: At the breaking point of the past and future, active in the now. Few other moments in life afford one the opportunity to recognize the now more than when the bittersweet taste of the end and the stomach-turning feel of the future meet. Recognizing the now is a blatant disregard for complacency, it's the subconscious desire for change realized, and if we're bright enough not to let us pass us by, it's the moment we experience life.*
>
> *So here I am. Third in line for take off, sitting in a not-so-spacious window seat, off to the sky to watch the gridded land and Lite Brite earth below me, moving westward. I love situations in which I'm metaphorically and literally doing something. I don't see how you couldn't. In this case, flying away from the past, defiantly going to meet my unknown, and realizing this transition is my life.*
>
> Or not.

It appears that I am, as they say, full of shit. On my return flight home from California four days later, I re-read my journal entry and could only shake my head at how big of an idiot I am. I met up with the artist, and he was a nice guy. The neighborhood was great, San Francisco was unbelievably beautiful, and all signs were pointing to yes. So of course, I said no. I still can't put my finger on what caused me to hesitate. Not knowing what to do once I got there? Was the move too fast? Too far? Maybe it was a little of all of these things. But I can't help thinking that I let myself down.

Back at home, I'm out on the porch reading the Cliff's Notes for *Hamlet* (of all things) and I'm struck by Goethe's interpretation of the hero, namely, that he suffered from an "overbalance of the contemplative faculty." During opportune times to act, Hamlet weighed the pros and cons so heavily that he caused himself to remain undecided until the moment was lost and he could relapse into thoughtfulness. I re-read the interpretation and my hypochondria kicks in. Is it possible that I suffer from the same thing? After spending all this time since graduation, weighing everything out, I finally feel I have a renewed clarity of mind in terms of where I'm headed, and yet, here I am, on my parents' porch, reading Cliff's Notes, starting to second-guess myself again. Have I missed a perfect chance for change just because of my constant uncertainty? Gah! It's the first time I've cursed Cliff's Notes for being so thin because all I want to do is hit it over my head repeatedly.

I toss the book under my chair and sink into a pensive mode. Tapping my thumbnail against my front teeth, I create a little beat to accompany my thoughts. Looking out at the front yard and the barns across the street feels like staring at a big painting and I imagine frames surrounding different parts of the view. Each time I frame a new part of the landscape, the picture looks like something I've seen a thousand times before. A truck by the gas pumps, wooden crates for squash stacked on top of each other, the grass of our lawn, which has actually grown pretty tall. I'm shocked no one has mentioned the grass. I frame a zoomed-in picture of the grass in my head and continue to tap at my teeth.

An artist named Robert Bechtle paints huge pictures that from far away look like simple snapshots blown up and framed for a museum. His paintings are of cars, or houses, or other everyday things like a having a drink at a barbeque, or a family standing together. He paints the scenes that you might have never really noticed if someone hadn't thought to take a quick photograph. The unexciting pictures that people quickly flip through when looking at old photo albums. And if they were only photos, Bechtle's work might not be so powerful. But because he paints with such amazing detail, the quiet scenes and ordinary moments that he captures are enhanced and become complex almost immediately.

In an article about Bechtle's work, Peter Schjeldahl wrote in *The New Yorker*, "Life is incredibly complicated, and the proof is that when you confront any simple, stopped part of it you are stupefied." That's exactly how I felt when I first saw his paintings. Stupefied. That's how I feel about this time spent at home, about the mental whirlwind I've experienced since graduation, all of it. Moving home after school slowed my life down to something so simple that I was absolutely flummoxed whenever I tried to make sense of it. Feeling frozen inside old snapshots of home, my family, and the everyday non-events that I'd seen a thousand times before, I became dazed by my own life. That's how I feel right now as I stare at the lawn and tap at my teeth. I'm sifting through thoughts once again when what I really need to do is just shut up and move.

The French doors to the house are open and I hear my mom calling from the kitchen to come grab a sandwich. I'm inclined to believe that people who make you sandwiches without being asked have your best interests at heart. She knows I've been upset with failed attempts to start something and the sandwich is the "Everything's going to be OK" speech that she knows I don't want to hear. Putting pretzels inside mine for that necessary crunch, we take our snack back out to the porch where we eat in silence.

My mother understands that for me, silence is just as large a part of conversation as talking. So while the sound of crunchy pretzels is the only noise I make, she knows what we're discussing.

As I'm appreciating the stillness of the day and the tastiness of the sandwich, my father rides by the house on a tractor yelling, "Do you want to mow the lawn, Jess?" He continues down the road and my mom and I look at each other for a minute before laughing. Shaking her head, she asks, "Why is it that everything in life is nothing like a television commercial?"

I'm not sure if I understand exactly what she means by it, but something tells me it is the smartest thing she's ever said to me. It serves as the doorbell for the "Everything is going to be OK" conversation that I eventually let in.

"Look, Jess," she says, "I know it's hard. When I was your age I followed steps. I finished college, I married Dad, and I started a family. There are a million different steps and none of them are wrong or right. It just takes time to figure out what works best for you. And that it takes time is probably the hardest part. It's hard to be your own archeologist; dusting things off, chipping away at others. But you'll find it. And if you don't, you can always live here forever and mow the lawn for your father." She smiles wryly before taking another bite of her sandwich.

I'm confident that this is the best advice I've ever heard. So instead of taking two new bags of pro and con over to the Scale of Consideration, I decide to pack a few big bags and book a one-way flight back to San Francisco. Maybe it will be great, maybe it won't, but I am through thinking about it. Sudden changes are often what make our own stories worth telling. If I keep overanalyzing every move I make or don't make, I'll never get anywhere. If action is the enemy of thought then I have to move, if only to stop the overbalance of my "contemplative faculty."

On this flight out, there was no ridiculous journal

entry. I simply sat staring out the window thinking about this incredibly bizarre dog-eared chapter of my life story. And it struck me that hey, maybe this is life. Maybe you just go out there and try to start something for yourself. Try to find a job, try to pay some bills, and then fill in the off hours as best as you can. Try to have some good laughs and some good loves so that you have something to think about when you're staring out plane windows. I sat and thought about the weird roommates I was leaving; their habits, the food, the volume control issues, the arguments, the blank stares. And I genuinely wondered how anyone does anything without the support of a few weird people.

****

When I arrived in California I stayed with a friend in Berkeley for a few days while I searched apartment postings again. I ended up finding an unfurnished bedroom with avocado-colored walls in an apartment above a crepe shop in SF's Cole Valley. The smells from the restaurant made the entryway hall smell like eggs and strawberries. It was the first apartment I saw on the first day I set out to find one, and I signed a check immediately. It just felt right.

The neighborhood is everything I had hoped for in terms of coffee shops and views, and there seem to be an unnatural amount of cute dogs everywhere, which is totally cool by me. There's a great little cheese store around the corner from my building that makes amazing sandwiches, Golden Gate Park is nearby, and I'm within walking distance of the single greatest record store in the world. My street is relatively silent save for the roar of the N-Judah train that runs outside my window every so often. The noise reminds me of the tractors and trucks from home and I've decided it is one of my favorite things about the apartment. Plus, I love the people-watching opportunities that come with having a train stop right outside my window. People look like true versions of themselves when they wait for trains.

One of my roommates is originally from Philly and within the first fifteen minutes of meeting him, he dropped a *Seinfeld* reference so I liked him immediately. I've noticed that when he watches television he laughs very loudly at all the jokes. I've never seen anyone laugh with so much verve at old reruns of *Cheers* or *The Daily Show*. I can't help but smile every time he does it. It's like having a laugh track or a live studio audience in the living room. My other roommate apparently spends a lot of time away from the apartment so I'm not sure when I'll meet him. I'm sort of hoping he's one of those characters that people talk about but never see. That might add some mystery to my living situation.

Waiting for my mattress to come in, I spent the first night in my new place on the living room sofa watching *When Harry Met Sally* wrapped in a comforter I bought at a Marshall's in the East Bay. When you move across America with only the bags that an airline will allow, you're forced to start anew, buying things that will serve as the starter set for your life. Attempting to create permanence and the idea of home out of temporary things like random lamps from Target, a desk I found at a stoop sale, and things I'm unable to assemble from IKEA. I have three leftover pieces from an IKEA nightstand that I put together, so I anticipate that falling apart any day now. But the excitement of the start makes all these things seem amazing. It's funny how a slightly tilted nightstand all of a sudden seems incredibly significant to me. If I were Robert Bechtle I'd paint a huge picture of my cheap, poorly assembled nightstand, just so I could always remember what trying to put something together feels like.

Moving to a new city is like having a baby—unless you've actually had a baby and then I suppose it's nothing like that. But everything is fresh and exciting and inspiring. With each new discovery, you feel the need to tell everyone about what your beautiful little city has just done. Walking around or at the most unexpected times, your city constantly surprises you. And while other cities are nice, there's just something so special about yours. Note: A city really isn't your own until you find a hairstylist you trust, schedule a teeth-cleaning with a dentist, and have someone at a locally owned small business know you by your order. I have a theory that everyone in the world wants a nickname, so if someone at a coffee shop or restaurant calls you by a nickname, you can rest assured that your city is yours.

But the love affair with a new city only lasts until you start to run out of money and then curse your city for being so damned expensive and demanding.

Leaving my parents' home has added immediacy to the long held thoughts of needing a job. Suddenly food stops restocking itself in the fridge and the calendar calls out that rent is just a few short weeks away and I think, no, seriously. I need to get a job. This is a crucial moment of honesty that pushes my generation into the workforce. Without the, "No, seriously" there would be a lot of well educated 20-somethings still asking, "What's for dinner?"

Searching for jobs online again is like meeting up with an ex who I know will break my heart. But here I go, thinking maybe this time things will be different. Applying to the tried and tested film jobs, I widen the scope to look for anything that offers a paycheck and think about an appropriate cover letter.

Dear Potential Employer,

I like eating and would like the opportunity to continue doing so. This job would afford me the chance to buy food, which seems nice. Please feel free to contact me at your earliest convenience. If I don't hear from you by the end of the week, I'll be forced to eat the leftover piece [13b] from my nightstand.

Thank You,
Jessica Martin

While looking through the myriad of postings I come across one with the title, "Room Service Order Taker At Luxury Hotel." Hmm, that seems pretty obvious, I wonder if there's more to it. After reading the description I conclude, nope, exactly as the title might suggest.

I have a friend who believes everyone has a magic power. Nothing extreme like flying or invisibility (those are super powers) but a magic power like knowing what month people were born in, or what they will choose to order in a restaurant. I'm inclined to agree with her that everyone does possess some sort of keen perceptiveness. My magic power is predicting ludicrous situations. Whenever I encounter a crazy person on public transportation, I can pinpoint with almost one hundred percent accuracy who that crazy will talk to—and it's usually me. So I suppose a stipulation to my magic power is that I can predict ludicrous situations for myself. A job called "Room Service Order Taker" is just ridiculous enough to be perfect for me. I send my résumé with confidence that I'll be called for an interview.

Days go by without hearing any word about that job. I pass the time by continuing to apply to postings online and by enjoying every second of the scavenger hunt involved with living in a new city. Collecting take-out menus from restaurants within delivery distance of my apartment, finding the grocery store with the cheapest cereal, testing out various movie theatres to see which one I will frequent, and trying to decide if I prefer to run in the park or on the track at Kezar Stadium. I've eaten a burrito almost every day and look forward to eating many more in an effort to figure out which taqueria will become my favorite. And I've discovered a dryer at my neighborhood Laundromat that gives ten minutes for a quarter instead of the usual six. It's a small technical glitch, but I found it on my own, and it makes me feel local.

NICE PANTS, SISYPHUS

The work of the world is common as mud
Botched, it smears the hands, crumbles to dust.
But the thing worth doing well done
Has a shape that satisfies, clean and evident.
Greek amphoras for wine or oil,
Hopi vases that held corn, are put in museums
But you know they were made to be used.
The pitcher cries for water to carry and the person
for work that is real.
    -To Be of Use by Marge Piercy

So I got a job. Finally. When you hang around anticipating something for an extended period of time, like a package lost in the mail or a phone call concerning a job, it's confusing to know how to react once it arrives. On the one hand, you're thrilled to receive whatever it is you were waiting for, but then again, it certainly did take long enough. It's the excitement to bitterness ratio many adults use to gage their happiness when they feel conflicted about waiting so long. If there is more excitement than bitterness (as is usually the case when a delayed appetizer is brought out to your table) happiness ensues. If the bitterness outweighs excitement, people stay pretty upset (see: every domestic flight terminal in America). The day I received the phone call concerning the Room Service Order Taker position I had applied for, I didn't have enough time to consider my ratio. I was in too much of a rush trying to find pants.

I should explain.

A few weeks ago I woke up to an unknown incoming call on my cell phone. Vaguely aware of the possibility that the call might concern a job, I cleared the sleep from my voice by testing a series of professional hellos before answering. I was tempted to answer with an English accent because hands down, that is my most professional sounding voice, but I thought that might be false advertising.

After introducing herself, the woman on the other end of the line explained that she had read over my résumé and wanted to meet me for an interview at the hotel that day before noon. Trying to maintain my professional tone as I rolled over in bed shifting books and water bottles away from my alarm clock, I saw that it was already nine o'clock. In all my brilliance during my move to California, I hadn't packed a single thing to wear to an interview, so I knew I needed at least an hour to go buy something. We agreed on a meeting time of 11:30 and I jumped out of bed to shower and head downtown to buy an interview outfit.

I was able to locate an Express with relative ease but was amazed to see so many other people in the store at such an early hour. My frantic search for pants was made infinitely more difficult given the sheer number of shoppers browsing through the mall at ten in the morning. What were they all doing there? Maybe they all had interviews too.

Buying clothes for work at stores like Express is almost a rite of passage for young working America. We don't talk about it but everyone does it, and it's a silent little clue that let's everyone know we're in the same boat. Like the dry-erase board for the door of your freshman dorm room. It wasn't discussed, it was just common knowledge that you should have one. Buying moderately priced, surprisingly well-cut pants at Express is the equivalent to a dry-erase board for your career track. It's just what you do. And maybe after you land that first job, you can start thinking about a pair of pants that every other girl your age doesn't already own.

I took a quick sweep around the store wondering what sort of clothing item would scream, "Hey, look at me! I'm qualified to take food orders over the phone!" A t-shirt with that written on it probably would have done the trick, but perhaps it was too literal. I decided to go with a nice pair of pants, my heels, and a button-down shirt: The classic go-to entry level outfit.

I picked out three different shirts and started looking for pants, but noticed all of the long lengths were gone. Because of my height, I usually have to go to a Zen place in my mind when I'm shopping. For some reason unknown to me, short girls love to buy pants that are clearly too long for them. The rational side of me says it's so they can wear any heel they want and pretend to be tall. The side of me that hates to shop says it's because they like to piss me off. Normally I end up agreeing it's a combination of the two and then think about a basket of puppies eating ice cream cones so that I can shop without ripping long pants from the hands of short girls. However, due to the time crunch for the interview that day, a shopping Zen was impossible to achieve. At one point I started trailing a small woman, asking to see the sizes of the pants she was holding. She pretended not to hear me.

Tearing through racks and shelves looking only for longs—colors and patterns be damned—I couldn't find any. I felt a pang of anger in the dressing room as I tried on pair after pair of what felt like Capri pants. It should be noted that pants are not meant to be tried on in a hurry. My experience in that dressing room felt like a Physical Challenge on *Double Dare* as I tried as quickly as possible to shimmy in and out of multiple styles of short pants.

I ended up settling for the longest pair I could find, resolving to wear them ultra-low on my waist, and buying a longer shirt to tuck in for coverage. I asked the salesgirl if I could wear the outfit out of the store and she reluctantly agreed, having me lean over the counter so she could scan the clothes and cut security tags off me. I placed the clothes I had worn to the store in a plastic shopping bag and figured I could check that bag at the front desk of the hotel before my interview. It would be a great first impression. "Hello, I have an 11:30 interview. And could you please hold this bag of old clothes for me?"

Before heading to the hotel I attempted to put earrings in for the first time in months. I thought I remembered reading somewhere that those holes never really close, and that's what I told myself as my ear started to bleed. Shrugging it off as adventures of a working girl, I walked through the streets of San Francisco's Financial District with extreme confidence. I had been waiting for this moment for a while. Head up, smile on, ear bleeding, my inner dialogue ran strong.

"Oh, hey there, don't mind me, just on my way to get a job. What do you think of the shirt? Exactly, I thought the other one was way too literal."

Even in my head I'm horrible with small talk.

Then, like any other time I've had even a hint of confidence, my heel became wedged in a crack in the sidewalk and I fell. I've had enough experience with this to know that falling in public is never good. But remembering my ultra-low rise (read: pulled down) pants, I was mindful as I fell that there was a strong possibility my ass was hanging out for all to see. Pulling the back of my pants up with one hand, attempting to break my fall with the other, I said a one-second prayer that my shoe wasn't broken and tried to play the whole thing off as a stretch.

For the coordinated people who have never experienced the pride-stubbing public fall, let me just say that the fall itself is never the worst part. The worst part is gathering yourself post-fall as you replay what you must have looked like falling, knowing that everyone around you is replaying it too. This is when I started to sweat.

Prying my heel from the jaw of the urban walkway I started to sweat some more. Wiping my face only to be reminded of my bleeding ear, I continued to sweat. Realizing how much I was sweating, I pulled my pants back down to make them seem long enough for my legs and tried to think of anything other than perspiration. This, of course, is the Stay Puft Marshmallow Man of perspiration, and the problem grew worse. Finally I told myself that tardiness would be far worse than sweat so I picked up my pace and made it to the interview on time.

Sitting across from my interviewer in the plush lounge area of the hotel, I was distracted by the well-dressed business people rolling their well-packed carry-ons through the lobby to the guest elevators. All the guests and employees at the hotel moved so fluidly. Their movements were quiet and graceful and everything was done with an exaggerated slowness as if they were walking at the bottom of a pool. I had to consciously fight shaking my head and rolling my eyes when I thought about how I must have looked in comparison. Bleeding, sweating like some sort of sweaty animal (pig, I guess? Are there others?), and attempting to form impressive answers to questions like, "Are you familiar with Mini-Bars?" How does one answer that question with more than a simple yes?

Taking a cue from the slow-moving opulence around me, I inhaled deeply before answering so that all of my responses seemed deliberate.

"Yes," I said, nodding slowly. "I *am* familiar with Mini-Bars."

The details of the order-taker position were explained in full and the phrase "Needs Anticipator" was dropped about fifteen times. For some reason, the term made me want to burst out laughing. Every time the woman interviewing me said it, I felt the corners of my mouth turn up before I quickly forced them down, giving me a nice facial twitch that I'm sure complimented the rest of my look very well.

She walked me through scenarios that arise during an average day on the job and tested my responses. If a guest's order was late, what would I do? Someone staying at the hotel couldn't eat wheat, how would I handle that? When an order for a burger left Room Service, what would I ensure was on that table? The answer to that last one was ketchup. The answer to most of these questions was ketchup. Whenever I mentioned a condiment she scribbled a note at the top of my résumé. What could she possibly have been writing? Job candidate knows what soy sauce is? I thought of what my potential business card might look like and became overjoyed with this option:

Jessica Martin
F&B Needs Anticipator
"I Know You Need Ketchup Before You Do."

The woman continued talking and I quickly glanced down at my pants, noticing that with my legs crossed, the cuff was about ten inches above my ankle.

"We cater to elite guests," she said. "Elite guests with particular tastes. So let's say for example, a guest doesn't want banana chips in his granola. We're going to pick those out for him. We're going to anticipate his needs."

"What an opportunity to shine behind the scenes!" I replied, feeling my face quiver.

She continued, "This job isn't limited to taking orders over the phone. You'd be involved in all aspects of room service."

"Well that would be wonderful," I said, shifting

slightly in my seat and pulling the pant leg down as far as I could.

Between the sweating, the facial ticks, the line of questioning, and the length of my pants, I had never been more uncomfortable in all my life. But two days later I found out that the job was mine, so I suppose it was all worth it. I really felt like writing the Alumni Association at Syracuse to let them know the big news.

Dear Alumni Association,

Thanks for everything. I'm currently asking people what
they'd like in their $16 omelets. If any graduates are looking for networking contacts in the field of over the phone breakfast inquiries, please feel free to give them my information.

Sincerely,

Jessica Martin
Room Service Order Taker

Prior to starting work I attended a two-day orientation to learn the mission statement of the hotel, its policies, and goals. Two days of sexual harassment seminars, overviews of benefits, a lot of poorly made videos played and PowerPoint presentations viewed. My fellow new hires and I were given a policy handbook chock-full of acronyms and after a few minutes of reviewing that I became convinced that companies are more thrilled with the acronyms they invent than the actual policies themselves. It's always the big finish to a presentation and each letter's meaning is explained with great fanfare. "It spells out **SERVICE**. Do you get it?!" Truthfully, there's an acronym to help you remember nearly every part of your day short of something for the restroom.

WASH.

We
Always
Soap
Hands.

I'm shocked they haven't thought of this one yet.

We were each given an acronym list guide that included thirteen acronyms. Isn't the point of an acronym to consolidate what you're trying to say? If you need a reference sheet for your acronym, maybe it's not as catchy as you think. Why not use one big acronym? Oh, wait, you mean like, **RASADASOLOR**? After a run through of all the acronyms, this mother of all acronyms was unveiled. The acronym created so that we might remember the other acronyms. This is for real.

Recognize
Acknowledge
Smile
Assist
Direct
Answer
Say Please
Ownership
Listen
Offer
Record

I sat looking at the sheet and jotted down my own acronym. **YGTBFKM**.

You've
Got
To
Be
Fucking
Kidding
Me

Granted, it wasn't English, but I'm sure Bjork has sung about it at some time or another.

At a certain point during the orientation I began to think only in acronyms and started breaking down everything people said into some clever word play. It was **HORRIBLE**.

The first day of orientation began with breakfast at the hotel's restaurant, which was incredibly nice, but served as a quick reminder that I haven't even scratched the surface of maturity. Our food was accompanied by miniature ketchups and Tobascos and I had to fight every urge to scream out, "Look how cute these are!" to the General Manager who was seated across from me. And it was incredibly difficult not to launch into a Larry David diatribe about the toast holder on the table.

When the toast was brought out in the toast holder (as far as I know it doesn't have another name) I stared at it for a solid minute. I thought I'd seen something like it before in *Gosford Park* or another movie where servants bring out toast in special holders. The idea of serving toast—which seems like the most simplistic of prepared foods—in a designated holder made almost no sense to me. It's toast. It's not a flame and gasoline. It's OK if pieces of toast touch each other. A toast holder seems so horribly unnecessary. If necessity is the mother of invention, how did that conversation go?

"I would have saved that man's life but I was holding this toast. Wait a minute…Holy crap! I have an idea!"

Staring at my separated toast, I realized that I never wanted to become a person who could eat breakfast without noticing the holder, like it was natural for the toast to be standing that way. To overlook the toast holder is to reach such a heightened level of obscurity I feel it would be impossible to relate to human beings. The luxury hotel industry rents used beds for thousands of dollars to people who will not think twice about their vertical toast and my job was to

141

anticipate that they'll need jam.

****

Time at work passes in that bizarre way that is simultaneously painfully slow and incredibly fast. The last twenty minutes before I leave each day seem like an eternity, but when I look at a calendar I can't believe that months have passed since I started. Having worked at the hotel for quite some time now, I can safely say that my job is a joke. I don't mean to minimize the work. The service industry is incredibly tough and all of my co-workers have elevated service to an art form. Truly. During breakfast rushes the cooks and servers fall into a dance-like rhythm of methodical movements, gliding around the kitchen effortlessly. They maintain steady hands and pace while carrying steaming hot stacks of covered food to trays and tables that they've brilliantly set up to accommodate all of the juices, coffees, fruit plates, pastry baskets, and morning papers. And no matter how many insane things are happening down in room service, the servers greet every guest with a warm, calm smile and a soothing tone that perfectly shrouds the chaos. I'm in awe of how good my co-workers are at their jobs. As for me, I'm not so great. So I guess I might be the biggest reason why my job is a joke. But maybe people who use college to write papers about the existential themes of movies like *My Dinner With Andre* should end up with joke jobs.

My job is to answer phones that never stop ringing and as a sound sensitive person, I now have a minor form of Tourette's because of it. Every time the phone rings I tell it to shut the fuck up before answering in an overly saccharine voice that makes me sick. I'm required to give a lengthy introduction of, "Good morning! Thank you for calling Room Service, my name is Jessica, how may I help you?" but most people cut me off after good morning, barking their order into my ear and hanging up before I can ask my mandatory up-sell question of, "And what type of freshly squeezed juice would you like?" It's a real treat dealing with the privileged public.

I have a theory that you can learn almost anything you need to know about a person through one of three things: What they find funny, how seriously they take board games, and how they treat people in the service industry. Working in the service industry, I've become a lot more sensitive to that last one. I think it might be the most important of the three.

Because I am so often ignored by the people I'm actually speaking to on the phone, my job seems pointless. If we can put a man on the moon, I'm sure someone could figure out how to order food through press-button options. But then there would be no one to yell at, and basically the main reason why positions like "order-taker" still exist is because rich people love to complain about their food. They just love it. They can't help themselves. They love to call and tell me that their latté was warm, not hot, they love to hate on the hollandaise, and they *love* to mention a missing item in their order. They're paying a lot of money to stay at the hotel, I get it, but some of these people don't even have a toe dipped into the pool of reality. I had a man yell at me for nearly five minutes over the phone because he didn't receive his bran muffin. As his voice grew louder and more irate, I sat holding the phone away from my face wondering if I had ever envisioned this kind of life for myself; if I had ever thought about showing up to work to have a man scream at me about a muffin. No, I decided. I hadn't.

The entire housekeeping department seems to view me as a *Ripley's Believe It Or Not* display, asking me constantly about my height. "Oh, very tall!" "How tall? How tall?" While I speak almost no Mandarin, I can pick up on subtle hints that tell me when my height is being discussed. On the service elevator one morning, I was surrounded by mostly tiny Chinese women and heard three minutes of furiously fast Mandarin followed by, "WNBA." There was a two-second pause before the entire elevator erupted into laughter. Little hints.

If I'm not answering questions about how high I can reach or having a housekeeper turn me around so we can stand back to back with each other, one of my Room Service co-workers ensures that each day is still an adventure. There seems to be a communication problem between us and it offends him when he feels he is being misunderstood. I can relate to his frustration, except that whenever the miscommunication occurs he screams at me.

"Jessica, watch out for him. He kills ladies."

"Sorry?"

"HE KILLS LADIES!"

Pause.

"You mean he's a lady killer?"

"THAT'S WHAT I SAID!"

"Jessica, Minnie Cooper is staying here tonight. Do you like her?"

"Sorry?"

"MINNIE COOPER!"

Pause.

"You mean Minnie Driver?"

"THAT'S WHAT I SAID!"

When I first started working I thought he was joking, but now I'm not so sure. I'm terrified to ask him to repeat himself. One day I thought he was saying my name so I just kept nodding and smiling at him. It turned out he was saying pasta.

I'm convinced the room service manager either hates me or thinks I'm an idiot and there's a strong possibility it's both. She often calls me Erica and speaks to me as if I've just come out of a coma, talking slowly and with a tone that sounds like she's hovering over me as I lay in a hospital bed. Anything she says to me sounds like a variation of, "Hello? Can you hear me in there? Do you know where you are?"

"Erica," she'll say, "can we talk about how you're folding the napkins? You're getting there, but look at these napkins over here. These are perfect. Can you fold perfect napkins too? I know you can. Do you have any questions?"

I'll shake my head no and when she turns to leave, I'll stare expressionlessly at nothing.

I employ Martin Freeman's blank stares about five times a day. Freeman played the character Tim in the BBC version of *The Office* and his inhales and vacant looks into the camera basically sum up my days at the hotel. In order to get through my eight-hour shifts I've turned to staring into cameras that aren't there.

One day when I came into work my assistant manager confronted me as soon as I walked in saying only, "I can make this card fly!" With no room to simply walk past him I decided, fine, I'll bite.

"What do you mean?" I asked.

"Look," he said, holding the card out for me to see, "normal card, right? But watch!" He then proceeded to toss the card out in front of him and it spun, suspended in mid-air.

I had three options here. The same three I'm faced with on the daily:

1) Fake amusement.
2) Fake interest and ask questions.
3) Stare into non-existent camera.

In order to maintain a working relationship with my co-workers, it's always a 1/2 combo and then maybe 3 when I find myself alone.

As I watched my boss spin a card around his body for a few minutes, I debated running out of the building, but settled on 1/2.

Me: Hey! How'd you do that?

Boss: Magic!

Me (Thinking): Yep, this is my superior.

Me: No, for real.

Boss: A magician never tells.

Me (Thinking): Right, but you're not a magician.

Me: OK, don't tell me.

Boss: No, OK, I'll show you.

So he let me in on the magic, which turned out to be a super fine string with wax on one end attached to the card, and the other end was taped behind his ear.

Boss: Cool, huh?

Me: Yea, but that means you've had that string taped to your head since—

Boss: 11:30. I didn't know when you were coming in.

I was scheduled to start at 3:00. So my boss taped string to his face for a little over three hours to impress me with a floating card. When another guy I work with came in about an hour later the Assistant Manager said, "Hey, look at what I can do!"

And before the card was even tossed, the server swatted at the air and ripped the string off his head saying only, "I know that trick" before walking away. That server has worked here for a while.

When not a career, a job is a job, is a job, is a job. Anyone working a job knows this. You become aware of the bizarre habits of co-workers, you shift into mind-numbing eight-hour routines, and you try to remind yourself that this is all temporary, hoping that the strange old man you see walking around your office didn't at one point say the same thing.

There's a man I see every now and then in the employee cafeteria to whom I'm always saying hello but never receiving a response. I'm not sure where in the hotel he works, but it couldn't be front of the house because his re-

fusal to speak wouldn't really fly there. When various sandwiches were served for lunch last week, he and I were the
only two people in the cafeteria and I watched as he picked
the bacon off every sandwich and ate it. He had to know I
saw him. I just think the effects of working under fluorescent lights for 20+ years made him not care. But that's what
a job is. It's watching random people eat all the bacon off of
sandwiches.

It's also showing up to things like the open-enroll-
ment meetings for health insurance and listening to your
co-workers discuss personal medical problems in front of
everyone. In retrospect, it probably wasn't a good idea that
I showed up to that meeting. As soon as they mentioned
Death and Dismemberment, I felt the urge to burst out
laughing. Obviously maturity issues come into play, but I
found it hilarious to think about how I might be dismem-
bered by answering the phone. And they went on and on
about all the benefits and bonuses you get from accidental
death on the job and I thought to myself, well that'll be
great. A nice fat lump sum of money will do me a lot of
good when I'm dead. But when I started to think about how
I could be killed answering the phone, the urge to laugh
faded slightly.

The health meetings are just a waiting game for the
dumbest question. I don't know why people feel compelled
to share personal information at these things, but they always do. I just sit there and shout inside my head, *The woman up front is an insurance agent, dummies! She's not a doctor!
But keep 'em coming because we're all getting paid OT to sit
here, or more, if an eye gets poked out or we die.*

On the dental section, the agent started to discuss
oral surgery and how if it's very invasive you can sometimes
use both dental and medical coverage to pay for it. Or something like that. I don't know. I wasn't really paying attention
because I knew people were waiting for her to finish so they
could talk about their mouths. She had already made clear

in the medical presentation that she wasn't a doctor. She HAD to be a dentist.

And sure enough, as soon as she asked, "Any questions?" hands shot up in the air. The restaurant supervisor started asking about a dental procedure she had just had. Literally. She was speaking in mumbled slurs because she still had stitches in her mouth. Inside my head I screamed, *Dude. Any question you're about to ask is too late.*

A bellman sitting next to me raised his hand and started complaining about an old crown, asking what he should do about it. I felt a tingle in my nose that told me I was about to start crying if I didn't laugh soon.

Agent: Well, I couldn't answer that, sir. You'd have to talk to your dentist.

Bellman's thought bubble: *You're not a dentist?! But my tooth hurts real bad!*

Bellman: But do you think the PPO plan would cover that? Even if it looks like this?

And he went on to open his mouth with a large smile to expose all his teeth, and I turned to look at him the moment he did this, and I couldn't help myself. I burst out laughing. Just me. Not even the Aetna agent. She must get stuff like that all the time. I quickly stopped laughing and made awkward eye contact with the bellman who probably thought I was laughing at his mouth—which I was—but not because it was bad, just because it's funny when people open their mouths for no reason and ask the dental opinions of those giving PowerPoint presentations. But that's what a job is. It's watching bacon-eaters ruin sandwiches and staring into the mouth of a bellman at required company meetings.

All of this might not apply to those who are passionate about their work, which, I believe, is the actual American Dream. To invest your time in something that gives you a personal feeling of achievement and pays you. That's the dream. I'm trying to work out how suggesting breakfast meat options to people over the phone figures into my dream. I haven't come up with anything yet.

Once in a great moon I cover mini-bar shifts, which consists of dragging around a half-ton cart of snacks and re-stocking guests' mini-fridges. I had an entire day of training for this. Seriously. I can finish the job in about three hours but I'm scheduled for eight hours and want to be paid for all eight. So after completing my tasks on mini-bar days I just find different hiding spots around the hotel and read the paper, helping myself to a $5 can of Pringles.

Have you ever had one of those moments when you are bitch-slapped with clarity? A moment when you look around and are nearly blinded by the absurdity of your situation? And in order to stay calm, you tell yourself that it's OK, this isn't really your life? That experience is my life. I clock in and out of that experience five times a week.

It hit me one day as I was bending down, checking mini-bars that, oh, I'm checking mini-bars. Enjoying some inner dialogue to help pass the time, my reality sat on me.

"Hey Jess. What'cha doin?"

"Checkin' mini-bars."

"Oh yeah? How do you do that?"

"Well you go into a room, open the fridge, look inside, then you close it. Sometimes you put a Coke or water in there. And then you hide for five hours."

"So it's kind of like being a doctor, or a lawyer, or a teacher, huh?"

"Yup. Only instead of being anything like those things, I restock $11 jars of cashews."

"Wow, so you must have gone to school for this, huh?"

"Well, not for this specifically, but I did have a mini-fridge there, so."

And then clarity walks along and I wince a little.

My situation isn't unique. Just like 8:00 AM lectures and public urination seemed out of the question in

149

college, sometimes you had to do both. And young people work random jobs that astound them because sometimes, that's just what you have to do. Marx had some good things to say about this. I've had some inner dialogue with Marx on slow mini-bar days. He'll raise some points about the alienated worker and I'll get all steamed, but then he'll start to eat the last of the Ghirardelli bars I need for the snack baskets so I'll have to ask him to leave.

It's best for my mental health that I don't work more than one mini-bar shift a month.

When I work as a server all of my nervous tendencies are heightened. I've discovered that I'm an absolutely terrible server but I attribute this to my work environment. Delivering food in room service is nothing like delivering food in a restaurant. The presentation of the food and wine is similar but in room service, the customer eats naked. The first time I delivered food to a naked guest I screamed in his face. It was honestly the last thing I had expected to see. When you're holding a tray of dim sum and a random naked man answers a door, your initial reaction is to scream. I'm sorry, it just is. Since that initial experience I've learned not to scream but the situations never grow less awkward. Setting up braised beef short rib dinners for couples lying in bed naked together was never revealed in the fine print of my job description.

People can be freaks when they stay in hotels and anyone who has ever worked in a hotel knows it. There's a tray on the service elevator used to hold miscellaneous items and one time it was filled with about seven dildos. Not knowing the Chinese translation for dildo, I looked with widened eyes to the housekeeper in the elevator and pointed to the tray. Before stepping out at her floor she just flatly said, "Lost and found." I suppose it was silly of me to expect a better explanation.

The worst is serving people my age or young pretentious children staying with their parents. One night upon delivering hot chocolate to a young boy staying with his friends in a room adjacent to his parents' suite, he asked in the most condescending tone, "Is this your job?!" To which I replied, "No. I'm an eccentric millionaire. I do this for fun." And then leaving the room, I softly added under my breath, "Fucking little shit."

But anyway, the mini-bar and serving shifts are few and far between so for the most part it is an order-taker's life for me. All of my experiences, all the books I've read, the places I've traveled, the people I've met, have led me here: to a tiny box of an office talking to people about picking raisins out of their cereal. On slow days or when the hotel has low occupancy I sit in my office just off of the kitchen and look at the floor, trying to understand what I'm doing with myself. My rational voice usually chimes in with something like, "You're paying off your student loans and getting health insurance like responsible people do all the time." I'll agree and feel better for a minute before my regular voice interjects with, "Or you could say that you're staring at the floor waiting for the phone to ring so you can talk to a stranger about salad." The latter voice always resonates.

It's hard not to feel a bit like Sisyphus as a Room Service Order Taker. Do you remember the story of Sisyphus? He was punished by the gods to perform the same task for all eternity: to roll a large rock to the top of a mountain, only to have it roll back to the bottom every time it reached the peak. I have that same futile feeling with my work. The phone rings, I answer it, take an order, and hang up. Repeat. Eight hours a day, five days a week. It's a rock of a different shape but the basic premise is the same. Everyday I go into work, the phones ring and I answer them. Next week the phones will ring and I'll answer them, and next month the same. There's never an actual end to it. There's never a final product, nothing that I can point to on a shelf years from now and say, "I helped make that." It's just day after day of answering ringing phones, rolling my rock, waiting for people to decide what they want to eat.

When I learned the story of Sisyphus in grade school, my teacher focused only on his ascent. She explained his fate by describing in detail the torturous task of pushing a heavy rock up a mountain forever. But in his *Myth of Sisyphus*, Albert Camus examined Sisyphus through his descent back down to the rock. He described the descent as the time Sisyphus was allowed to consider his situation and when he became aware of his fate. By fully acknowledging the absurdity of his fate during his descents, Sisyphus became superior to it. Camus called Sisyphus the absurd hero because even after recognizing his absurd struggle, he was able to find happiness within it. Just as Oedipus, who after realizing the tragic turn of events in his life was able to declare that, "all is well," Camus believed Sisyphus could reach the same conclusion. He says of Oedipus' declaration, "That remark is sacred. It echoes in the wild and limited universe of man. It teaches that all is not, has not been exhausted."

I have to remind myself of this every time a guest spending $2,600 a night on a room yells at me, or whenever the phone rings relentlessly for three straight hours, or any instance in which I need to apologize to a grown adult because we ran out of their favorite cheese. I have to remind myself that if Sisyphus could find joy in the descent back down to his rock, the very least I can do is try not to swear at the phone every time it rings.

During the height of my Sisyphean existence at work, the hotel announced a mandatory seminar for all of the employees, hosted by a motivational speaker. This was bad news. When I hear the words "motivational speaker" I think, "Van down by the river." I think conductor-instructed clapping to make a group of people sound like a rainmaker. I think of different places I could hide instead of listening to someone pump me up about Room Service Order-Taking. But alas, there I was.

The speaker began by telling a story about a girl

with no arms who volunteered to pass out books to a class-room of students. One by one the students took a book from under her chin and this was the speaker's metaphor for the service industry. Hi, exploitive? What type of freshly squeezed juice would you like?

She passed out ribbons to each of us (using her arms) that read "I Make A Difference" and shared the story behind them. The idea for the ribbons started with a teacher in California and slowly spread across the country. The concept reached New York where a teacher gave a ribbon to all her students and one of those students gave the ribbon to his brother, who gave it to his boss at a law firm, who gave it to his son, who broke down crying because he was going to kill himself but didn't because his dad had given him a used ribbon. I sat at my table in the banquet room with my head slightly tilted, thanking the woman under my breath for sharing that lengthy mass forwarded email with us. I would be sure to pass it along to one hundred of my closest friends in five minutes so as not to have bad luck.

I started to zone during the last twenty minutes of her talk but somehow we all ended up sitting around wearing Elvis glasses with attached sideburns, telling each other why we make a difference. If this woman motivated me to do anything it was to stand up and scream at everyone, "What are we doing?!" But of course I said nothing. I just sat quietly and listened to "Suspicious Minds" play as my dignity sneaked out the back door to hide.

It's this cosmic trap I'm caught in, forever searching for universals, only to be completely mystified by the ones that keep popping up. I'm just now starting to realize that the inexplicable situations in which I keep finding myself are the universals. In college, out of college, employed, un-employed, at home with my family, or out on my own, I'm surrounded by absurdity and rewarded with happiness by recognizing it. What else is a girl to do?

Have you ever seen footage of a baby giraffe or deer

taking its first steps? These early times in our lives are no less humorous. We're all pushing for success and happiness (just don't ask us to define those terms) and maybe we're working fantastic jobs or maybe not, but if there is a fear of uncertainty in our future, we'll let someone else say it first. Because we're in a "Hey, I'm walking!" mindset even though we've yet to fully establish our footing. We've all got the look with our shoes and our dry-cleaned suits, and we ride trains downtown with our earbuds in, pretending it's only us and our playlist, which is just as unique and unusual as we are. And we're on our way to work, where we're off to make a difference, only we're not sure what that is exactly because we forgot what **D.I.F.F.E.R.E.N.C.E.** stands for.

I was thinking about this yesterday on the morning train, crammed up against strangers, shuttling off to do whatever it is we do to keep this crazy world spinning. When the train moved underground I caught a glimpse of my morose 8:00 A.M. window reflection and noticed that most of my fellow riders shared the same expression. Sisyphus came to mind immediately. Readjusting my grip on the tiny bit of pole I had been allowed, I looked around the crowded car to see if anyone was smiling during our descent to the rock. But with well-groomed appearance, everyone just looked down or to their coffee, so as not to meet eyes with the person exactly like them to their left. Failing to recognize our similar situation on that train, our similar situations in general, we were all missing out on life's ridiculous beauty. Checking off life goal lists, forcing tidy ends to our tales, believing that there is an order to it all, we ignored the faces on that morning train told us otherwise. This life is messy, and untied, and strange, and for as predictable as it may seem, none of us really have a fucking clue what's going on. And if it doesn't seem that way, you're just trying too hard to avoid it.

My observation on the train was interrupted right before my stop when the girl standing behind me tapped my shoulder.

"Excuse me," she said. "You're on my pants."

Moving my feet quickly I turned to apologize. "Sorry about that."

"No worries," she said. "They're just too long."

Getting off the train and walking up to the street where I waited for the illuminated man to tell me to move, I laughed to myself.

Nice. Long. Pants.

And maybe that's the most we can hope for. Those unforced smiles that remind us all is well.

ABOUT THE AUTHOR:

Jessica Martin grew up on her family's farm in Brockport, New York. She spent her formative years talking to herself in the mirror and memorizing lines from *Full House* episodes. She graduated from Syracuse University with a degree in Television, Radio and Film and that proved to be worthwhile in that she still enjoys all of those things. After living in San Francisco, New York, and Boston, Jessica has learned the importance of light layers, irony, and remembering how people take their coffee.

A fortune cookie once told her that she finds beauty in ordinary things, and she liked this. But then another fortune cookie told her that she liked horse racing and gambling, but not to excess, so she's not entirely sure what to believe. She sort of thinks fortune cookies should stop pretending they know her so well. Her daily musings can be found at openeyedsneeze.blogspot.com.

Open-Eyed Sneeze is her first book.